S0-BLU-216

Doppler Effect

JOHN KINSELLA is the author of over twenty books, including *The Hunt* (Bloodaxe/FACP, 1998), *The Hierarchy of Sheep* (Bloodaxe/FACP, 2000/2001), *Auto* (Salt, 2000) and *Peripheral Light: Selected and New Poems* (W. W. Norton, 2003). He is editor of the international literary journal *Salt*, consultant editor of *Westerly*, Cambridge correspondent for *Overland*, and international editor of the American journal *The Kenyon Review*. He is a Fellow of Churchill College, Cambridge University, Adjunct Professor to Edith Cowan University and Professor of English at Kenyon College.

Also by John Kinsella

Poems
   Peripheral Light: Selected and New Poems
   The Hierarchy of Sheep
   Zone
   Visitants
   The Benefaction
   The Hunt
   Poems 1980–1994
   Graphology
   Lightning Tree
   The Undertow
   The Radnoti Poems
   The Silo: A Pastoral Symphony
   Erratum/Frame(d)
   Syzygy
   Full Fathom Five
   Eschatologies
   Night Parrots

Fiction
   Genre
   Grappling Eros
   Conspiracies (with Tracy Ryan)

Drama
   Divinations: Four Plays (edited by Stephen Chinna)

Autobiography
   Auto

1495

Doppler Effect

JOHN KINSELLA

Introduction by Marjorie Perloff

SALT

CAMBRIDGE

PUBLISHED BY SALT PUBLISHING

PO Box 937, Great Wilbraham, Cambridge PDO CB1 5JX United Kingdom
PO Box 202, Applecross, Western Australia 6153

All rights reserved

© John Kinsella, 2004
Introduction © Marjorie Perloff, 2004

The right of John Kinsella to be identified as the
author of this work has been asserted by him in accordance
with Section 77 of the Copyright, Designs and Patents Act 1988.

This book is in copyright. Subject to statutory exception
and to provisions of relevant collective licensing agreements,
no reproduction of any part may take place without the written
permission of Salt Publishing.

First published 2004

Printed and bound in the United Kingdom by Lightning Source

Typeset in Swift 9.5 / 13

*This book is sold subject to the conditions that it shall not,
by way of trade or otherwise, be lent, re-sold, hired out,
or otherwise circulated without the publisher's prior consent
in any form of binding or cover other than that in which
it is published and without a similar condition including this
condition being imposed on the subsequent purchaser.*

ISBN 1 84471 020 3 paperback

SP

1 3 5 7 9 8 6 4 2

for Lyn Hejinian

Contents

Acknowledgments

Syzygy was originally published by Fremantle Arts Centre Press (1993). *Erratum/Frame(d)* was originally published by Folio/Fremantle Arts Centre Press (1995), while *The Radnoti Poems* (1996), *Graphology* (1997) and *The Benefaction* (1999) were originally published by Equipage. Acknowledgments are also made to the journals: *Angel Exhaust*, *Antithesis*, *Boxkite*, *CCCP6*, *cordite*, *Electronic Poetry Center*, *5-trope*, *fragmente*, *Imago*, *Jacket*, *Meanjin*, *Metre*, *New American Writing*, *Pequod*, *Picador New Writing*, *Salt*, *Siglo*, *Southern Review*, *Sulfur*, *Takahe*, *Talisman*, *Thumbscrew*, *Tinfish*, and *Verse*.

Erratum/Frame(d) is dedicated to the memory of Tristan Tzara, *The Radnoti Poems* are dedicated to Fifi Radnoti, *Graphology* is dedicated to J. H. Prynne. *The Benefaction* is dedicated to Susan Howe; extracts from an early version of *The Benefaction* appeared in *Redoubt* (1990).

"Naff or Language signifiers are fucking boring" is from *Pine*, an email collaborative text compiled with Keston Sutherland and published as a chapbook by Folio (Salt), Cambridge 1998. *Alterity: Poems Without Tom Raworth* was originally part of a collaborative work with Tom Raworth. Tom extracted his poems for use elsewhere, so I collected mine in a chapbook under this title published by x-poezie, New York, 1998. *The Cars That Ate Paris: A Romance* was published by the American Association of Australian Literary Studies for its seventeenth annual conference in Kansas City. "Transgenic Pig Ode" originally appeared in *Discourses*, edited by Jo Shapcott, published by The Royal Institution of Great Britain, London, 2002. Some of the "Echidna" poems are from *Zoo*, published by Paperbark Press, Sydney, 2000. The Echidna poems were written for Jacques Derrida. *Sheep Dip* was published by Wild Honey Press, Co. Wicklow, 1998.

The Ern Malley Poems started life as a solo project, then became an interaction with John Ashbery and later involved John Tranter.

Each poet channelled Ern in his own way.

Thanks to Tracy Ryan and Rod Mengham for supporting this work over the years. And thanks, Chris, for your patience and hard work.

Introduction: A Mythology Reflects Its Region
by Marjorie Perloff

John Kinsella, everyone seems to agree, is a phenomenon. Born in 1963 in remote South Perth in Western Australia, Kinsella has already published more than a dozen collections of poems, including the 1998 Bloodaxe collection *Poems 1980–1994*, which runs to almost 400 pages. He is the founding editor of the important Australian journal Salt (which has now branches out so as to publish books as well), was a guest-editor of the multicultural journal *Kunapipi*, has edited little magazines, poetry features, and anthologies, and has participated in collaborations with artists, photographers, and fellow poets. A Fellow of Churchill College, Cambridge as well as a professor at Kenyon College in Ohio, Kinsella shuttles back and forth between the UK and US, with stints in Australia in between. By his own account, he doesn't sleep more than two or three hours a night because there are so many important things to do during one's waking hours. Indeed, Kinsella is perhaps the first poet to dwell mentally in cyberspace: wherever he happens to be in actual time and space, he is emailing around the world, sending poems to friends and editors, receiving the work of others, and participating in dialogue about poetics, linguistics, ecology, and politics. And the irony of this cyber-existence is that Kinsella is first and foremost a regionalist—the celebrant of a very particular landscape most of us have never seen. Like Yeats's Sligo or Hardy's Wessex, Kinsella's south-west Australian wheatbelt has already taken its place in the imagination of the young twenty-first century.

Now Kinsella has put together a volume of his "experimental" poems that runs to some 422 pages. In Kinsella's case, it's hard to tell which of his poems are and which aren't "experimental." *Syzygy*, to my mind the most innovative in the group selected here, also appeared in the Bloodaxe *Poems 1980–1994*; other sequences like *The Benefaction*, *Alterity*, and *Graphology*, dating from the later nineties, have appeared as small-press chapbooks, as opposed to the more mainstream collections of "counter-pastorals" (Kinsella's own term) found in *The Silo* (Arc 1997) and *Visitants* (Bloodaxe, 1999). But the division between "mainstream" and "experimental" is, in Kinsella's case, largely arbitrary, the main value of *The Doppler Effect* being that we now have before us an exciting body of work culled from chapbooks and uncollected manuscripts many readers will not yet know.

"Experimental" is a word I have come to dislike, given its overuse today, when every new artwork or piece of writing or musical composition is quickly hailed as "experimental" and then just as quickly forgotten as even newer "innovative" works arrive on the scene in what sometimes looks like an orgy of commodification and replacement. But John Kinsella's poems, whether small press or in the Bloodaxe collections, really are experimental. Not so much in their form: on the page, Kinsella's free verse is not markedly different from that of other Australian or, for that matter, British poets of his generation. Sometimes he uses stanzas, ranging from the couplet to the sonnet, sometimes he writes prose poems and sometimes, as in Tarot, each of the ten poems is a fourteen-line square, made of capital letters. But primarily Kinsella's poems are organized into long, loose free-verse columns, whose words and phrases are collaged together, avoiding normal syntactic markers.

"Experimental," in Kinsella's case, is not to be confused with language poetry. True, he has obviously learned from Lyn Hejinian (to whom this book is dedicated), from Susan Howe (see Graphology), from Steve McCaffery, whose paragrams have echoes in some of the minimalist poems in Syzygy, like "peine forte et dûre" (#18) and "gloat" (#19), and from the complex language games and poetics of Charles Bernstein. But unlike these and other Language poets, Kinsella is not quite willing to suspend disbelief, to allow for uncertainty and indeterminacy. For someone as ecologically aware as is Kinsella, someone who has strong feelings about the despoliation of Australian lands and the killing of the indigenous peoples, negative capability, Charles Bernstein or even John Ashbery-style, just won't cut it. Thus, when Kinsella experiments, as he sometimes does, with the paragram and the pun, producing lines like

By re-active blood/y
Mis-fortune
Assigned Con tra Dik shuns
("GLOATS")

the cut-ups and new spellings (as in "Con tra Dik shuns") don't create double or triple meanings as they would, say, in Steve McCaffery's work, and thus these particular experiments may be construed as somewhat gimmicky.

No, the real experimentalism of Kinsella's poems, especially the more recent sequences like *Sheep Dip* originally printed as a 3 × 5 inch mini-book with a sheep on its cover (Wild Honey Press, 1998), that looks as if it should belong in the childrens' section until one reads the fine print of its 21 pages of four-line stanzas, has to do with tone and vocabulary. Kinsella's are true post-Romantic and post-Modern poems in their strange impersonality. Even when this poet uses the first-person—and he generally does—his lyrics lack inwardness; their momentum is summed up in Wallace Stevens's phrase "Not Ideas About the Thing but the Thing Itself." At the same time, these counter- pastorals or anti-lyric lyrics are hardly Imagist or Objectivist, their vocabulary being so arcane, so scientific, and specialized that they remind us that "nature imagery," that staple of English verse from the Romantics to the Georgians and beyond, has now been replaced by the X-Ray, the MRI, by echocardiography (a prime example of the workings of the Doppler Effect), and hypertext.

Thus, in the first few pages of *Syzygy* [from the Greek *suzygos*, meaning yoked or paired, whether in conjunction or opposition], we meet words like *kraken, bathysphere, paperbarks, pellagra, tragacanth,* and *cacology,* and *inquiline.* A reader, especially a non-Australian reader like myself who doesn't know that a tragacanth is "a gum used in the manufacture of pills and adhesives, in textile printing, and as a stabilizer in thickening sauces" or "a plant from which tragacanth gum is obtained, especially a spiny Asian plant with white, yellow, or purple flowers," must read Kinsella with the dictionary close at hand. And yet, Kinsella's knowledge of the zoology, botany, and geology of his native Western Australia is so profound, that his introduction of *tragacanth* or *paperbark* ("an Australian species of tree with pale thin papery bark that peels off in large sheets") is never merely wilful or exhibitionist. 'Writing the pastoral now, here," he says in his recent on-line "Essay on Pastoral," "one must be ironic and (consequently) political. The ecologic conversations between shepherds have become those between motorbikes and tractors, helicopters and light planes. Even the climates are changing. Greenhouse Effect, ozone layer, etcetera. Nothing is consistent and consistency is what the pastoral has always been about."

In this context, the anatomy of lake and swamp plants, rocks, asteroids, and chemical waste that we find in Kinsella's poetry may be understood as a twenty-first century version of Wordsworth's declaration that "To me, the meanest flower that blows can give/ Thoughts that do often lie too deep for tears." What Kinsella understands, perhaps more powerfully than any other poet currently writing, is that the urban/rural dichotomy most poets subscribe to is a false one. True, most of us now dwell in urban or suburban environments and the city, via malls and shopping centers, keeps encroaching on the landscape around it. But "nature" is just as important and just as "real" as it ever was for the English Romantics, only now the "natural" world, even in the furthest backwater of the Australian continent, bears the imprint of a century or more of human intervention and contamination. This may be a common enough thematic motif of Green or eco-poetics, but Kinsella really makes it new.

Consider the opening of #5 of *Syzygy* called "The Cane Cutter"

Reflex take a breath. ( ) A snake
operates amongst rough cane-cutter's crystalline sweat.
A particle overload.
Heavy rain bearing down

palpitating trifoliate with sun and cane
no rainbow
makes an appearance.
Earthy very earthy. Miasma
camouflaged mud takes all takers
and throws back a marsh of fences.
They beg for tariffs. They like restrictions.
In the highlands water is lightning
gaping press-down and half bas-relief.
Turbine churn-out comes down
from highlife where the air is heady.
No fireflies there. Dowsed and riddled
deep deep south roots dry the bone-black
subterranean streams, raddled shapes forking azurine
on meeting archaeological light, spent swarming
the traps, for this is Ground Zero Warholing
in cyclone territory, zoning the sirens
equivocating hot dogs and pies mushrooms
pushed to the side of the plate: cadillacs
racketing Monroe hubcaps
currency cut like love
on a breezy day, hot air concentrating
in the sewers.

In physics, the *Doppler Effect* is defined as "an increase (or decrease) in
the frequency of sound, light, or other waves as the source and
observer move toward (or away from) each other. The effect causes the
sudden change in pitch noticeable in a passing siren, as well as the
redshift seen by astronomers. This definition applies neatly, not only
to such thematic "Doppler Effect" sequences as *red shift / blue shift*,
which follows Syzygy in the new volume, but in poems like "The Cane
Cutter." The poem begins as a description of cane cutting in the
remote swamps, the "reflex tak[ing] a breath," as a snake is spied in
the grass. It is evidently rough work, given the bursts of heavy rain
alternating with sun, the latter obscured by the cane itself creating a

"trifoliate" pattern that blocks out the possibility of seeing a rainbow. So far, the poem is descriptive—a nature scene. But with line 8, the *Doppler Effect* begins to occur. For where is the reader positioned vis-à-vis the cane cutters? Where is this "miasma"—this poisonous emanation caused by decaying organic matter that looks like "camouflaged mud"—coming from? Evidently there are industrial works close by so that this seemingly "rough" landscape is one of fences, tariffs, restrictions—of "Turbine churn-out" that "comes down / from highlife." Having to cut cane in this world seems like pure hell. "No fireflies there." On the contrary, a lot of hideous waste matter, coming down from "bone-black / subterranean streams, raddled shapes forking azurine / on meeting archaeological light." What horrible pollution has taken place in this once pristine landscape? We only know that it is "Ground Zero," the term originally referring to "the point on the surface of land or water that is the precise site of nuclear detonation. But "Warholing" suggests that here "ground zero" is a serial act, a repetition with slight variation as in Warhol's silkscreens of Campbell Soup Cans or serial images of Jackie.

And now the scene turns surreal. Is the problem natural (cyclone) or man-made (sirens)? The scene has shifted imperceptibly from the cane forests to the contemporary world of hot dogs and meat pies, "mushrooms pushed to the side" of dirty paper plates and "cadillacs/ racketing Monroe hubcaps." How did the reader come from the cane world to this disgusting scene where hubcaps are bounced back and forth in the asphalt jungle? Here it is not cane that is being cut but "currency"—the money paid for the "products" imposed on the landscape. And the "hot air" that caused the "cane-cutter's crystalline sweat" is now "hot air concentrating / in the sewers."

Kinsella details all this without direct commentary: the poet seemingly stands outside the scene, a mere recorder of "events." But each verb and adjective is charged with meaning, so that the image of rot, decay, stagnation, and false progress" explodes in the reader's mind. Alliteration, as in "cane cutter's crystalline sweat," and internal rhyme as in "Zero Warhol-" define the scene. But what is most important—and this is consistently the case in Kinsella's work—is the absence of people, even as the human is inserted into the life of things by means of prosopopeia and transferred epithet. Take those "raddled" shapes of line 18, pointing back to "Dowsed and riddled" two lines earlier. "Raddled" means "worn out from a life of indulgence." By calling the stuff that floats up to the surface of those polluted streams "raddled," Kinsella gives us a powerful image of a world where the very geology speaks of human corruption. No "love" in this fallen world, only "racketing Monroe hubcaps" and "currency." Farming—with its cane-cutting activity—has become the victim of the "turbine churn out" that has turned earth, grass, plants, and trees into a sewer.

I write here as someone who is by no means an environmental activist and who must plead ignorance about the daily life Kinsella describes in these graphic, surreal, and painful anti-pastorals. Painful but also exhilarating in that the poetry brings the fallen world of Perth—and its analogues wherever they may be—squarely into the reader's own discourse radius. Here is a section of Canto 5 in the aptly named sequence *Graphology*:

the tooled vinyl
evokes the odour
of a Chevrolet flat-top

in the Avon valley,
South Western Australia,
the post-Mabo lysis

strung up in the courts,
the racist graffiti
on the Kelmscott bus stops

the diminishing exteriorization,
as dimensions decrease in the hastily
applied scrawl; moving inland

substantial horizontal
movements of air
morph sand paintings

while snakes twitch
on the hot, fluid fields
of silica.

There are those snakes again, right in the path of whoever is "moving inland" in that Chevrolet flat-top. The picture falls into place and we're all in it.

Syzygy

1 APPREHENSION

And how did you feel
the surface too close
and the flappers fizzing
at your tender
and vulnerable
                    feet
loaded with misgivings?
Swift overload catapulting
recrimination
the largess culminating
cinema papers boys-own-annual-ing
from post office to mailbox
and bicycle-clip braces
on the maligned bull terrier's
teeth: an island of green
reticulated sucked into the soft pink
of the suburb, insurmountable the ratepayer's
anguish and bravado! the house a kraken
or bathysphere undercutting the plane,
adjunct to surface, one dimensional
suction. O fear ripples evading
sonar buoys Blue Gum Lake
receding as bores suck effluent
from beneath the arses of ducks.

Paperbarks turn black
water soils over
banks of sodden bread
and soft drink cans
this is popular viewing
medium small frame minutiae
chronic screen or inhabited pasture,
pointillist and contentious

cartooning serious ineptitudes
hatchback unravelling a bend
the lock-stock
barrelling it into sticky drink
at the bottom of the can: sure,
we feel strung up and depleted — light
even heavy and darkness uplifting,
necessitating remission into screaming
as the engine revs the flywheel
seems not to move dear o dear
love's texts spread haphazardly over the bucket
seats — and don't we know
they're braggarts! denying fusion
and invading asteroids, deploying
consumables and calling
it art.

2 FALLOUT

A refugee from contention I load
stills into the projector
taking the negative impression
adjuncting
expression prising anger
out of its folds
the damage budding retentive
small experiment releasing heat:
remember looting these impressions?
machinery expressive and light-
conscious love scarifying poise
the tractor rocketing the clods of loamy earth
bootlegging frustration mudbrick and fencewire
circular-saws threatening Robert Frosts
and doorpost jamming two years too old

and rotting, the sun orange plastic,
perfect, the film was black
and white and the sheep gurgling
hysterically.

3 Self-regard

-ing homonculous metals chambers
tinfoiling exclusions like humidicribs
wheeling slick asphalt deletions
and stripping film, dust water licking
axminster carpet spreadsheets—what shows
in the headlights or pinheaded
spotlight? Crunch. Synthetic victims.
And the frogs croak politely
in their ditches. HALT! Good year
wet weather halts the death of a zebra
just outside a butcher's shop. Can't read the signs
good who gives a damn anyway?
Needed, inquire within: good management
and sensible market indicators.
Those who leave anything up to description
need not remote opinions. Morality
stinks, we keep it in buckets.

4 When the flappers tickle your fancy

opposing needs, priming pellegra
with plastic cement like jelly rubber
singing aging movies, tall tales lugging drabness
out of forums: humitrophic, water glass
or sundial gas-bagging in the shade, Ah
such is fame passing the time. The car comes.

A stretch in tails. Silk doors predella
adjuncting talent AND the driver. Let us in!
Take us entire rhomboidal all and Oolala
susurrous through disconnexion, baffling
sibilence. O my flappers, what a team we make!
And the planets co-habitate and read life
impression, you have your strict
and your lax, the cups drink too much
and the television in the back of the limo
is stuck on the same channel. The driver
is sucking himself. Take no notice.
You are my family he splurges:
executors   guardians   trustees
receivers   inheritors
good sides half backs
flankers absorbers potentates
contrivers emissaries
agitators incarnations
lovers leaping onto the tired pile
of my flesh.

5 THE CANE CUTTER

Reflex take a breath. ( )   A snake
operates amongst rough cane-cutter's crystalline sweat.
A particle overload.
Heavy rain bearing down
palpitating trifoliate with sun and cane
no rainbow
makes an appearance.
Earthy very earthy. Miasma
camouflaged mud takes all takers
and throws back a marsh of fences.
They beg for tariffs. They like restrictions.

In the highlands water is lightning
gaping press-down and half bas-relief.
Turbine churn-out comes down
from highlife where the air is heady.
No fireflies there. Dowsed and riddled
deep deep south roots dry the bone-black
subterranean streams, raddled shapes forking azurine
on meeting archaeological light, spent swarming
the traps, for this is Ground Zero Warholing
in cyclone territory, zoning the sirens
equivocating hot dogs and pies mushrooms
pushed to the side of the plate: cadillacs
racketing Monroe hubcaps
currency cut like love
on a breezy day, hot air concentrating
in the sewers.

6 LIFE-DRIVER

Placating pit swimmers
the bone mill splurgers
credit cards bursting middle-class prognosis
dialectic good will and science
is upon us bursting prognosis
good will tragacanth
imprint forms lotus form
the new behemoth, a signature naked
beneath the ultra-violet: rex regis
suppressing atoll watchers, spreading
blood and bone over the garden. Lair-down devil
lair down! Vrooom!

7 SUBJECTING OBJECTS TO SERIOUS SCRUTINY

Draining absence as blue
trance stelazine melting circulars
　　　restraining the abstract
　　　fingerpainting
lithium to bind
Mono Mondrian on its platform of shape:
threatening construction on its very
printed page, corrector fluid
swashbuckling first words
formatted like a river ending
in a window mouse decorating
graphic disasters
without compassion. We impose.
Macrographic-Beta-Language.
And you don't even have to
drop names!
　　　　　Advertising blimps
nudge traffic controllers pneumatic
in their agitating seats,
tattoos green with red tracers
running like hits. Here, disasters
falsetto screech *sus. per coll.*
like corporate suicide
across the polished screens.

8 THE FOREST, THE FARM. A HYBRID BATHYSPHERE

Lumped or polyglotted, mixing
but insistent on claustrophobic
limits, cans of repellent
stink like flypaper.
They undercut a fluid market

holding back the fragile forest,
rending tight-as-money-talk, marketeers
would cut sleepers where they stood:
Chinese whispers like nostalgia. Downburnt
the weird beast charts pressure, breath
contrivance as the water is fire:
volunteers roll back the pasture, the forest
corals and suffers. Greenhousing
the coldest waters, peepshow languishing
amongst saw-jawed lantern fish
surface molten, stripped of its cage.

9 INFLECTING AMBIGUITY / ELECTRIC TRAINS

A type of ambiguity
that carves the hissing wires
clouds volcanic on the scarp
as kids general motor it with a mania
that drives them East: surveillance
a seance partially materialising
voices from closets steel-faced
and never changing critics
like having a field day: tracks glisten
briefly like sin in its rage
cauterising
                rugged-up patrons waiting
for concert tickets outside
the entertainment centre
as staunch pylons share goods and flashes
with cameras and country trains, not electric
but still photogenic. Dispensation
of tickets as curricles dash past
and we celebrate the past.

Palpable cacology—admit the document—
juggling heartburn
passing paludal intoxicants
adhesives and cleansing agents
out back the hardware store
supermarket strings strummed or struck
the plastic shopping bag dissolving
or blowing up like a lung,
thick and tumorous when breath whispers
triplicate super realist on super realist
zygal chevron zippered-up
the fire-escape rusted
and decompressed—the blossom
plucked while locked
in its cloak and cap, night-fruit
copping it sweet in daylight: our bodies
botanical: facades
as the tallest poppy
accepts the flak
its tinted window reflecting
it back, carbonaceous angels
triggering sumptuous sprinklers,
the housing estates sinking
into the swamp stomping
faddish death beats
only the well-heeled speak
borrowing cultural tid-bits
repackaged   tender   taste-sensitised
suppressing the threats.

11 DELETIONS

Fortitude rippling cross-sense-
a-round clip-board logic
accumulating detailing Harleys
like shepherd's calendars in the month
of January the heat was Cyrenaic and intense
displaced vermillion weathering
irregularities like windows
and quick assimilations, pique & niche,
lavender disaster soft and not in the slightest
mechanical—BUT deletion rakes
a monster making shape from less
than its constituents, well-made enigmas
propitiatory hermeneutic and well coded,
I differ camping on fault-lines highways upending
bridges siphoning rivers neuter
crushed velvet ripped from the dash,
die bobbing infra-red night sight slick like bedrock and pylons
congealed beneath town planners forgetting mud, acronym
comfortable city lazy body lay-about
the pool pretzels beer and much more: the 'staff of life'
single tracking compression and tidiness,
an accident absorbs clumping only
for publicity: obliquity luxuriant
first class dozer drivers machining silver spray
amyl nitrate staining fingers
in tills corporate gets-ya-goin' up and adam
furrowing nutrition and filling cavities.

Spontaneous bloodstock rattles and broods
lapping power-lifted pasture amidst
the fences — narcs and passive devourers of feed
immunising syringes. Meathood gestures gantries
and ramps while Soutine feeds love in a French
abattoir la la la B grade and trendy, rattle O three-tiered
calashes, looking brutal in the halogens, cauterising
debris up-ended white posts with red and silver
dazzlers lowering their lids, slipping on damp days
into the smell of wool and hide, mopping
placental blankets with rough tongues.
Window painting stretch addressing
ambulance and attendant starter motors
commensural commercial additives
like bolt guns stunning and electro-shock
on top of the hill beneath a liver-shaped moon
draining the blood from your nervous
system-ism, the spill-down lathering
the coronets of your contact-lenses, drainage inquiline
wearing it like a glove or
coating stomachs — STIFFEN UP LADS! the Hoi
polloi tax-evading and avoiding road-blocks
born into banking liquids that solidify
with limb-movement, the floor
approaching rapidly: a Gnostic
logion: the fish nibbles my toes
and good it feels sovereign vessels toes & lips
divisive
hobnobbing
traipsing stainless on the whetstone   outcrop
sheep-weather-alert
or battery-bound and the wind chaffing tinwalls
clocking the pulse of eggdrop and peelable wool

and udders performing ridiculous labours: supreme-O
a brand name marketable, affirmations corporate
conferring garnished parsley hints, staking
first grade glue sticks how many shares?
brokered on the floor household cleansers
banish the addictive canvas, Ah tundra vista
the canvas captures and projects
the sky shocked and hooked
Mrs McCarthy & Mrs Brown
immobilised by Tuna fish, disaster spread
like emulsified stabilised sheen upon
Marilyn's tender lips c/- Big Sirs: Sir
of the pigskin briefcase, brylcream quinella
stated portfolio lapses pump-action
and blood-staked, entablature
en-loading your own quizzing sense-around. Smell it!
Singing western and roto broiling I've hooked a big one
bone black and threatening to move
quotes like numerous grains of dry powder
centrefire monumentalised 1080
vacuuming heat-sealed trophies skins
pre-packaged mise-en-scene urging texture
out of quadrature, arc the brittle black
cuttlefish, sepia toning cinemas
flensing storage facilities, you drag
something up out of memory and into sight.
Steaming black frost cleansing sun deliciously sharp
and breakfasting on the damp patio, lush tallow
candle canopying shades and predicting a good
hard-humping sunset. Progenate policedog
physiology derived and detecting goals
evaluating hereditary from 'weaning to slaughter'
heterozygous random caracass the beauty
collapses, Santayana might have been ugly.

13 RIPPLES

Streaming blue divisions, sections
of the neighbourhood, the lights of Canning Vale
ludicrous sporting brilliance rainslicks
like the MCG and gracing a stadium of cages—
Movietone ships sink and planes disperse
in black strategy, walk-on parts erotically
developing & reproducing cryptic typologies;
passion active and unassailable, declaring
intermittently, rippling like the skin
of persons or sulo-bins rattled by traffic,
city initiated carnivale for officers
on chilly Autumn nights ekeing out nostalgia
clumped together at the same scene long after
the bang, roadgame, cosmic microwave
background radiation as the fighter plane
sends tracers spitting into columns
of uniformly spread refugees: organisation
saves none of them.

14 TRIGGER

Yoke the vicious integer, sun and moon
uncomfortably syzygetic: 'Deep Throat'
shifting consensus, plead your case
and get the hell out of here. I won't
listen anyway! The quadrature sets limits
AND appeals X pronto. Things don't stick
unless they're forced to. No couples
can sit comfortably here: rekindling
love-on-a-pier, the car humming
on a verge or aiming for the country
downwind and forgetful upending the heart

off-loading blots of anger a clock chimes
in a mall of pastiche. Trigger, I fall
collecting apogaeon multiples of disorder.

15 Landfall / The Collapse Of Beauty

Loose materials patterning sundials
at water's edge: embracing saline
trend/'/s crystalline fatigues
-loss- myriad system
-is-ation
interest vis-à-vis
disintegral compendiums, oil-slick
& refuse & foam casually concocting
beneath an historic swing bridge
a couple of hours [drive fro]m Perth, up-river
skiers hacking the lower
reaches
and paddocks might appear
mostly folds of beauty
—tourists understand this!—satisfying
rare inner-city creatures marooned
passive purposeful indulgently
headlines might claim.

16 Chemical

Boom-arm pod-fed nuzzles teaming foam
out over red earth: new machines
churning chemical seas in-lateral drift-a-round
phenomenally hand-in-hand with tractors
and deranged furrows rippling

heavy clods of soil

           run-off creek river sea

deranged furrowing residual

    when myth hits purchase

who wants clean food?

bulimic south anorexic mid-point

    dr i p-fed north

deep-inhaling flyspray

and mosquito coils

fr - ie - ze dried coffee

cleaning a particularly

stubborn stove or bad guests

from a party.

17 FIRST BLOOD

Tubed out of you warm and recycled cold.
Flow impedes logic cold as stain-
less steel like a disinterested object
of beauty, sun-bathing internal solarium
blood ultra'd & raddled
re: transfusion. Dizzy float extract
inflatables, double toxicological
cell-sized machines making repairs
restructuring walls disengaged
by injective inter-ex-change
blood money breathes
franchise fantastic voyage
efficient redistribution
for this they test. byo.
branching profusely
gaining the respect
of ambulance drivers
slamming T-bar automatics gloved

and averting, petrol-guzzling
monsters finned and beautiful
gybing through your sanguine &
unguent utterings
staunch against venomous
      '{Dais de l'oeil revulse}'
bathe five death on red/s: (a) disaster
guilt feud bath (h)ound letting lust sport
thirsty money-stained sucker
auspicate consanguinity
rarely colourless or violently positive
genealogy suppurating
my grandfather fell
into the offal pit: Benny's Bonemill
          circa
1923.

18 PEINE FORTE ET DURE

What pleads 'I',
in the gloom, of
bulb-blow
& ocean-carpet
closing shore
lee & lea
to hills
a sprinkle of desquamating quartz
          sun-dank
spent
                re-flex-ive
though who owns the fragments (?)

19 GLOAT

who   lives by
    lies by
and
buy re-active blood/y
mis-fortune
assigned Con tra Dik shuns
an audience despite their buying
    him drinks
pneumatics taxonomy dialectics
    & quark of despair.

20 FEEDBACK

Charles (O)lson
'Not one death but memor
    ot accumulation but change, the feedback is
the   aw

21 FUME

Soil tactless infuses
dust-cradles   *   objectifies
black frost on breathing land
fuming. anger military
pro fuse   Ion deficient
upper upper   flight
developing a dislike
for 'us': the bulldozers
have sweet tooths & fume.

22 FLOAT — ING

(I)

Respond
float-ing soil
heresy
and the fog
absorbs pink-quartz
thrust-drift.

(II)

Tractor churns heavy
despotic bones: sheep anatomy
undering edgy discs
and salty furrows luminous
night-work
driver's red-neck hurts.

(III)

Fencing wire coils
snakes complex
in gullies

crops
and wild radishes
rot.

(IV)

Scour stalk-base and stubble
vast rimmed fields
charred in waves,
ash-water lapping
like gout: first rains
float.

23 Narrative

(i) telescope: passive

Up in the hills / closer: week (end) tours
not the building you'd think
[though] they've made
the right moves in the foyer. The
predicate fails to leave, we assume
via adjustin gth efoca llen g th
that he's always been (t)here! Zeiss
optics.

(ii) the night sky might be an all day sucker

take down [to] flatlands the jigger
of nostalgia—a few slides lo-priority
& secure. they call him Kid. hey Kid
cop a load of the moon} loud in his
ear pricking with chilly air. it & the sun.
orange & blue.
his father's hand conjoin-
ing
with an ear
left spare.

(iii) the living planet

seeder/combine. re-building
rain-washed spreads. the water deleterious & demi.
And all they've got to say
Is what a wonderful vista!
Not city lights absorbing
The stars—even the moon
Looks (more) vivid. Taut.   here
Check out sun in summer's

                     centre
Comes the reply. I'll bet ya!
Cannot [any] lies well in randomness?

(iv) Expansion

lock stock and barrel
ie carrying its orbit in-
consistently.   Note: key words. access?
Proper
bucketing
they gave him.
Proper. and they've electrified the railway
as well.
what the hell, he drank his first wine
at communion. transfixed: Kid's re-
call.

23 NA(RRA)TIVE / *chapelle ardente*

Syz-23-key: uh oh
fetish or frou-frou
aza labels & ers on
artifize the case:
richter's rats struggle
& quickly
give up: identify. musical casing
setted. Up up up!

Rhe
-toric plans an
invest   atations & calendars: grey
gunboats sweeping
dank rainforest rivers. patrons
of calypse & stoker
the moon drums UP tides: awash
melt-in-the-mouth} riprap.
& drawn out. ra ra ra.

isotopies
Id di
possières
gestes
temps perdu tristan tzara
morphemic and trendy
up-
wards & categorise?

linger
mechaniser
'senex iratus'
swiftly
sits: progression towards

a system. Yes.
Yes.

logos
go go
& presuppose a % of
an *
[vraisemblance]
eschews a?

Touchy on a point
of picture & linkage = so what?
newstart with a kick
& get comfortable.

This case has potential: look,
they've got the drop
on you. De-
tailing
edifice &
scripture/s &
inspire-
ation: the sun brightens
            the shell grouting
            paving the lap lap
            of motoring stretched
            waves & sandbar circumflexed
            the pillars softly set
            and sinking, coming unstuck
            on soft-served banks, upwards
            & downwind the puckered hills
            glow like the haze. A fly
            settles on a fish corpse
and dies.

23.5 PANTOUM

souwester blows cold
ha ha says granma
you'll chill to the bone
out there on the water

ha ha says granma
we gotta anyway
out there on the water
that's where goes sun & moon

we gotta anyway
cold when it oughta be hot
that's where goes sun & moon
burst & mix with blue

cold when it oughta be hot
we saw it in the telescope
burst and mix with blue
burnt dark like the road

we saw it in the telescope
granpa let us look
burnt dark like the road
and too close to lie

23 LIFT

Ex hale and don't re-
(in) flate
        it's dark
when you go out
{ing}   the fires

[24]

retract wetlands
breath iced lakes
spoonbill & ibis
lurch-dance (in) space
{ing}   mongrams
   [memory] re-
call the day, the weight
of light-lift, roll-back
sun buoyant
sienna-&-orange   luff & clouds & hills
obsessive and
manic   *   prone to out-
bursts
de rigueur
Ah! not love neat on the bus
I see {thru} your window/face
                take
me back.

24 ON

Oh ON!   loosely
never held   pivot(al) sans
      desire
on degeneration c/- object in
NO! touch me. On.

25 URBAN CROSS-OVER

Your soy coloured teeth
moth dust skin dys
function
-al: redress:

just a question
of supply: all roads lead in,
supply: all your
working daze: shopping trolleys
con-joining
in car-
parks. Howzat?

26 RURAL PATRONISING

Trill & twee wagtail lift
little nervous
nell-ies
take a break
at the heart the header
moves out over good soil
rippling like radiation
an electric
storm
spiriting
up-lifts,
& the fear
of fire & need for rain.

27 INTERMISSION

I chase a hair
over my lip
trace it
with
tongue

& shiver spine deep and
hear my insides
recoil: a glass
to the wall!

28 REALITY

If it's real it's been photo-
graphed but not by lips
testing on recall cauterised
word(s)—slash & burn, scorched
earth realising opacity
of skin and smooth cool sight
in our hands, wounds
washed & THE LAND
never sulking.

29 LINK

Speech I link. Pro-
crastinate. 'Weialala leia'. Eh?
What did you say?
Can't make
head nor tail.
Of it: lyric?

30: RE (CON) STRUCTURE ING / DAMAGE
CONTROL

(a) Ponge c/- or à la Fahnestock

ah
'In this undergrowth, half shade half-sun
Who thrusts these sticks between our spokes?'

> river white burnt & scullcraft
> taunting drift downtide, down
> in the mouth & down towards
> the centrifugal drag, & towed
> & motored the sherry stained
> ramps, I cry & laugh and palpitate

& can

not right & moralise
& catastrophise & lies
out & about before sequestering
downs the spout & closes
the ment (al) gap: lash
out

                              no longer & yet
locate a shell of me like paving stones
zippy brass em[boss]-ing names
but not mine
god
willingly
the swells of pleasure lurid
& not a little jealous
of another era

                              seventy miles from here
                              where on lordly manors

clean hope
for forgiveness
but no more
blood below hook & rafter
becoming dirt

but
no more
cast in plaster
moulded joan   of arc   or jocaster
in revolutionary colours
caged & carved
                biblical
red velvet fierce companions
perfect
eyes are missing
cont-
          rol is
or has   been
dam(ag)ed:

> quartz or nacre
> lose lustre (less)
> minutiae
> packed & labelled
> analytic & rolling
>   fencewire
> plugging gulleys

certain
even

       lichen covered rags
scrunched & welded
ARE dead parrots
sauve-qui-peut
   (!)

The point of impact
fabricates & inde
pend {ates} enances — a disc plough
or slave cylinder
mixing mediums
with disaster
intra-personally: saltwash,
the creeks are storming
the river
& the crops are
waterlogged—melaleuka & salt scars
collaborate in a bundesfest
discordant
visits politely
call ING music
out-back. the tractor   ['wends its weary way]
no longer bushbashing
but superating spray
from soil, frisking
clean air
& tourists
warm in town   (as
                                         Uncle Gerry
                                         talks to Les Murray
                                         who compares
                                         Bunyah with

pasture
& a trio
of harmonists
make a go of friendship
without a tenor
providing a damn good

afternoon tea. You won't hear
cheques bouncing here. rather
sinking sand
& cockatoos.

& yes, we can hear the shutters
a-clicking & the chortle
of buses cruising down
the town's main street.

a stickler in a yella rain-jacket checkin'
the water troughs out in the rain
always wishing more sheep shelter
& the precise quantity & placement
of precipitate, as the tractor
sidles up to the silver fuel tank
& drinks.
this, I know. & re-
lease. the tractor is a star!
out here.

hot lead is introduced
to Crater Valley. Not True valley,
more of a deep deep creek between granite
and sandstone sweeps & high language shot & sheeted. crumble
lipping down to the York Gummed floor
& sheets split as sharp
as plough discs. of course.
For Crater Valley is also
The Valley of Foxes.
& they come, cousins & weekend hunters
& deplete.
& the need for locusts

as the third bell is raised
in its tower & God spits yellow
is begrudgingly ac-

cepted.

& earth-tear
(as) families quake
stationwagons, earth snake
deep down & ripping up

Alien

hatchling.   old barn down
and (the) wells drained:
fresh gullies
ground thunder

groundwater thunders (complete)

[33]

despair
backstroking cross-lane or cutting the windrows
of THE childhood nightmare   I look
to the STREET
for a % -age & Age
& free (of)
tracasseries/   replete

(b) & Ponge / Fahnestock:

     'As also for
grass to straw,
or to the calamus for writing

to the pipe of "inspiration"
(. . . and to the straw in the "cocktail",
in the tall glass of the "long drink")'

the '&' is OUR angel.

Eh, balance up
spreadsheet
& paint on the carpet,
selling out
& making my almost (self)
<clear>. Eh, SPEAK UP
with subtlety:
I'm here & your practising virtue.

Eh, SPEAK UP
I can't hear & listen too quickly:

> he shook the box
> and could NOT
> guess the contents.

Tractor parts.
Splinters from
THAT wagon wheel.
& a copy
of

POETRY

March 1966

Mary Ellen Solt: 'Flowers In Concrete'
'Magnificent
Aurioles
Rousing
Insensate
Grief
Oh
Long
Death
Suddenly'   #   here bottlebrush trees
drag blood out of cemeteries.

Red shift / blue shift

The Wanderers

Inclement the social weather
and cultural backdrop
barely palatable, as huge meat diets
taste local fair as if it were
process, the fetish
as determined in the mind
and not the passions: where mere
bourgeois functionaries
set documents in order
while nobler selves savage
hypocrisy without awareness,
this is depth as arrogance,
like preserving the tail
of a yellow-bellied skink
they've scared from its
sunning spot, tapered
nerves flickering like conscience
they blot out with righteousness,
sitting on piles of dirty money.
From country to country,
oppressed culture to another,
majority or minority
in the ousted Apocalypse.
We'll have none of that here.
As if one could remove the brain
and still not overcome
the genius {of it all}. Wander-
ing to something and knowing
it as imperative
as derivative
as expedient, all in appropriation
emancipating verisimilitude
of: hey, your abstractions
signifying nothing, soothing
the landed ache as if

from a seaside (no, greater
yet! THE OCEAN) mansion,
but of course it's fate
and a foil to the Academie!:
who gives a damn
about spelling!
It's like suspicion
or the grumbling gut
that masques as *Eraser-
head*, the Daddy-power
diminished in manifested
sperm. It's climatic,
inducing tropical
overtones, the fog
of similitude,
the dusty cradle
of civilization a teasing memory,
possibility? Who said:
"Science
is watching us."?
But then a wanderer
is never a woman
in the language;
lyrically they denied
their way down the <u>oath</u>way,
straight is the gate
so abhorred
it deflects intrusion. Up
North the belly dumpers carry
Dampier salt, the tides
move like nomadic hordes
in visualizations of Scythia.
It's idyllic at <u>Mill</u> <u>Stream</u>.
Once this continent
was connected to India.

[42]

Much later there was a landbridge
into Asia. New Guinea
and the North of Queensland
share(d) flora and fauna:
deterministic this singularity
against expansion,
polemic as redshift: they can't
get back now the seasonal
turbulence antiphonises
the clutterings of their palate,
read permanently
in translation
the land itemizes
excursions: like an artist's
diary: it's surprising
when a background
comes alive
like instigation, rumour
sourcing the point of infinite
malice like displacement theory,
all belonging to the very same
mass of festivity,
like Geryon polluting
(an) other's songs, like panels
set-up to amuse the gentry:
itinerant the learned
and wordly-wise, this
fellowship of wanderers,
serious
and grandiose
in their buffoonery.

The Doppler Effect And The Australian Pastoral

RED SHIFT

In memory it moves steadily into the red
as if the feathers of a Western Rosella
are blood, and time is the application
of heat to the seen, the fox moving with the rapid
beat of lightning coruscating the vermilion rim
of a constant daybreak or nightfall, dry thunder the applause
of a crowd crazy about the exits, as if towns squat
close to the sparking dirt, or dissemble into their
constituents through prisms of salt crystals,
and all of it moving away from you like
the fading drone of the water truck,
the receding dams, the shed skins
of black polythene pipe growing brittle
like the black expanse of an expanding universe
captured and defined, its escape realised,
plotted and planned, the bird traps set
on the periphery of the farm,
the increasingly rare birds
perishing as the property
changes hands and the hunters
forget to disarm the drought.

BLUE SHIFT

The rich blood of action
coming through like a bullet,
all birds with blue feathers
squawking at the top of their voices

as if the deeply blue sky
is the centre and all is thundering
towards it, the desolate expanse
a ruse, feigning infertility—

drought the cranky codger
who is at once a brown snake
and a racehorse goanna, or the creek
heavy with night, grotesque

and bristling with myth—
as if it's always been almost upon us
and we're just beginning to see
beyond the construct of history.

Terraforming

for Jeremy

A prey bird flies
       suddenly
cedilla in its grasp
with carrion anonymity,
thwarting pacts and boundaries
as cold fronts and accrued
       ordinance
encrypt with rumour;
the ruffled field a plough's scamming
profit in scannable lines of sowing,
       as legend or grand design,
pinpointing a subject,
       having the presence of mind,
the evolutionary
              tact to ignore
the glowing reports of order.

Emending context flashfloods

stipulate death as endgame,
field-mice washed-out & riding
the cracker-barrel towards
a fossil fame
an oily slime emerging
from the paddock's eroding side
patronising rainbows arched
over Needlings' pendulum
hills [filmy deviations
in colour]—the holiday
should have begun
a few days earlier
and then the sun
would have played dynamic
with hearts
and brooding juices.
On the extremities
Thomas Hardy
lodges heartily
indoors—vulnerable & sleeping
later than usual, sleep the colour
of burnished jamtree flesh
left on the salt flats
for thirty-three years,
whittled needle-sharp
and looking other-worldly.
O so briefly the sun pierces
and lifts the covers.
That freaky crosswind
exploits the rattle
of an approaching truck:
soon-to-be plunging
articulated vehicle
crashing axle-down
foul-mouthed & abusive

with washout,
the flooded cabin,
drainage overflowing
and cutting up
the driveway, intransigent
and committing atrocities
among the polished roots
of York Gums.

Saltweed
and lowland cut-a-way,
moving lines in burnback
and deeply red clay,
arched backbone—high above the core—
curves, infiltrates, and sets,
cools rapidly as the surface retreats,
as the forest lifts and the sky, a sheet of dry ice, slips
from season to season,
beating a hasty retreat
that is the defeat of mirages,
quenching light and knuckling down,
dismantling the crust
of the devil's Dante-esque flesh—
the flesh all fire and the breath vapour.
The backbone rests
despite its bed shifting
against the plains of Heaven, bracing
its imitation-perfect-joints, singing
whiplash against the painted rocks,
the fossils of its failures,
detractors from its triumph
on a continent of infinite variety
where civilisation is a dead bird that flies
against an inland ocean

ICons: ab-sence

I make no art
or facts
now

any more
would be
uncalled for:

idolatrous

the voiceprints
blank & al-
ready

waiting
as script
as

heavy as searching
be-low
an image, icon

framed
as paint-
ing or unravelling

titles
more than owner-

ship
the length
& breadth

Is imagination
or imaginings?
You must tell

us this, I have no speech
for the dialectic

of red/white, &
yellow
roses

the gardens
in Bloomsbury
full

& anagrammatic,
thorns papersharp
& eager

to write
their names
in exnominated flesh.

Sparklers, Hawks, & Electric Trains

The magnetic float
stylized
like in-form critics
plundering
sure bets
through respectable
media outlets.
Rolf Harris's stylophone
humms, whizzes, and buzzes
like a conspiracy
brewed in caves deep
beneath the Nullarbor Plain.
Which has something
to do with Americans.
The evidence:
a photograph,
fuzzy around the edges.
The electric train glides
silently
out of the station
and nails a dozen pedestrians
slickly to the sleepers.
The high voltage lines
hover overhead
like inimitable hawks.
Nobody can work them out.
But then sparklers
shape-shifting
in rail-side
backyards
divine
a brilliant future.
That much
            at least
is clear.

The Bridge Twists Like a Möbius Strip: A Lyric

The solar-acetylene torch
spots a shell of the opera house,
cloud-valves
opening cylinders and increasing
the heat. Viewed from a pier
the bridge twists like a möbius strip
while trains continue
in their slight
deceptive arc.
Across the ria
a deserted Luna Park
practises its mechanical husbandry
silently.

Tide Table

Oddly levelled diaspora
& flight I cannot be defined
it says, chromatic
as only a special camera
might capture
a tiger moth, amongst the linen
or imprisoned
in brilliant & solitary flight—
the tidal blood or necessary
flowing: that every diversion
wandering
sudden change in direction
caused by a predatorial threat
has been and will be written. The sum total of
all tidal leanings in the blood,
the nervous system,
gyroscopic
is love.

Lowflying the flood
or woodsmoke
in the burnt offerings
of past lives
or propositions
or hoped-for destinations.
We have arrived nowhere
but hope to move on.
The flood
the highwater mark,
shed like collective calling cards
or whirr and delays
C/- satellites,

whom about, about whom,
we circulate
but never orbit—that's gravitational
and the effort to break free
will damage this delicate
wing
structure.

I-deletion in the avant-garde space

Seen around the I are pterygiums
& cataracts, or near, in the orb
inside out, the minute particles
split from the avant-garde space,
parasitic like furriers reviving
in a dying market, or like I
depletions in the seeing
of the new, its potential
variation which is linear
time.
      The cost of the op
in a private hospital
is prohibitive, though not
critical if you pay
a premium level
of cover. You see despite not
being aware you've seen:
entering the light into your
corrected system, your inner sight
risen like an essay
on projective verse.
We see
collectively the night heron
indelible against
the photosensitive river,
a something collected
from deep within
the darkroom.

polytype

"A school of fish, not accepting the inclusion of water
In concept . . ."
CHE QIANZI (*trans* JEFFREY TWITCHELL)

They moved in the evolving countenance
like a street demonstration, missing in action
the blooming reportage, wave crests & troughs
    enforcing chapels on the fringes
    of tidy towns, the waterways
heavy-weeded and red-bloom algae succulent,
an indifferent ode to otherness, this whimsical
criticism of cells, obtunding this Matthew Arnold.

A right idea has no history, just punches
in the old time clock decorating the tessitura.
They heard him sing when IT was at its finest.
        Job security. A Titian. The Gypsy
        Madonna a fusion of non sequiturs
and false names. Low otherness of systems
they see and follow politely, dispersing memoria.
Too late on Etna Empedocles this gory discipline.

Technology is not in language. Murmured soliloquy.
Calque and gnosis: they saw you there leaning
casual against the mob, unloading your Nikon
      which subverts the throw-aways.
      Unless the plant is soulless. Un-
admit the feeling. In spite, the nourishing
as by word of mouth the sea grows sticky. Drinking
incomplete, as feeder & decay implicate the proper food.

As policy the open door contempts the verbal. The askance
of kingdoms lotused up & sold as image. They are
different there. There, they are, as they should be.
    In translation. Poise, the deep dry
    river bed can't stand the season, & the changes
come too slowly. Prose-lapse the pilgrimage. As fish eggs
blow like sand against the banks they walk in sequence.
Credit a potential phonogène; let's enjoy the silence.

Mirror script a practical science, in seventh heaven
they dropped a letter of base utterance, u ho, ho hu in the
crowded jokes, as if a linguist should drink too much,
   glossing ethnographies and writing-up as
   should be read. Oral emulations take essay
with deliverance as warping chases the quoinish furniture.
The point is to redeem the text as glory & joy. Finesse
the bordered register. Precise a slight hilarious dish.

in-discrete-harmonics
for Drew Milne

Serve the simple form
or spectrograph, direct-inking
deployed or posited expression,
mobbing the tongue's tuck
and tapping, informing
sun vocal on window-boxes,
and yes, they're watching.

Cant subsong component
in-chorus, speaking out
like balloons or banners,
quasi-tympanic and passive
in-canon: intrinsic,
replete with gutturals,
resonating in-senate.

Taken as law accuracy
variegates, a pied bird hesitates
about all music: releasing visual
purities and gutting harmonics;
it's locality and location and dust
on the larynx, deft parrots
talking up captivity—resonating.

Inwards: the weather

Thorn-dulled in the sheen
wellenbereich, reif
in the hoar blanc
ptica across the border
infinitive paziti
recontrer du mauvais temps
heavygoing de la turbulence
which isn't the sense
nublado in Coimbra,
if it would construct itself
as such: low chuva, in the
or under: chove a câbatros,
I'll take a break on that
like a worker come home
with the educated speaking
English late into the night/ ce sera
partie remise/ per tormenta
brewed, I thank you in Barcelona,
un torrente de injurias
in heavy weather as summer
refuses

hydrography

Obsessive reservoir ringing changes as dowser & hazel twig twist sharply
over water-way deep patterning flood plain mimicking a subterranean
hot spot in dry southern places damping family & stock & seasons of poise
designated drought or stream riveting bodies of water perennial corpses
diminishing a Pont Neuf flurry of mechanics as the gaudy fountain sprays
fashionable names in-font per vascular fons et origo, georgically gloating
weir a misshapen picaresque fattened on bloodworms scripted on tidal flats
innate down-stream, filaments flexing circularities & principles, beauty-flow
bent theatrical, red perch destroying status quo, changing habitats feeding
arterial pumps as empire drives its barge inwards from the mouth, large-bellied
black swan duping a wader's scurry compressing slurry occupation like
stacks in hyper-spatial flocks; text block on text block opening engravings
from Les Raisons des forces mouvantes: confluence, text & pre-history,
editorials inciting offshore inquiries into Cayman Island companies.

Natural Objects

"the gentle sway of natural objects"
"Michael", WORDSWORTH

relic of sedatives
back-burner days
now all marzipan—
convoluted with almonds—
poisoned refrain mumbling
for twelve days and beyond,
clogging perception per radial
ascerbations, high stunt alterity
fibulations, asserting you've
been here overeating
three-d, like snowflakes
or agitated traffic, casual bouts
and soap bubbles, for that's science
in a strait-jacket, free like
thinking. ho ho ho. compressed
core or ur-word, advertising
in the accusative—thee takes
the lesson from the reliquary,
leaving modulation of tongue
and nothingness,
rock candy

The Flowering

Not knowing the name
or living standards
of this plant
on the verge
of flowering —
I should call myself
an "impassive
observer" —
but something requires
more of me
than this — or seems to —
the soil in the bed
so dry, the sun
unseasonally warm,
and the bottle of water
I hold in my hand
half-full.

A Small Tornado

rot-a-ting up/
                    drafts
warm humid air vor-

text

        street corner San Francisco
where rev
                ellers, levellers
gravi-agitate religious
freedom, para-
tolerance & metem-
psych-or-osis, nyms
of particles & iculars,
acceler atial, rates & spin,
ergo integer photons
snap-shot, instantly developed
and album-ed:
counter heavy Greco-
heritance,
age,
arrested
on New Year's Eve
cylindrically
the taught cables holding the span
and through or under the super-power relaxes
as between
shed & house a willy willy kicks arse,
shaking up
drafts and scurry, scatter & puff
or jokes aside lacerating the softs of eyes,
slicker an un-used-t';
lash regard/less
trans, participation, perspiration,
precipitation in the tiff & tuft

up er, error
tracks all bent
trans continental
storm, located,
collatoral,
smart

Unabridged
for Katherine

Reading the mirror
as staged like a glade
or sylvan murmuring,
nature without engagement,
intra-dynastic spread of family
across the pages
of history—not shrinking
a big personality
to a character sketch, nor living
the good life and relaxing
into the storyline
while *What Katy Did*
and *What Katy Did Next*
condense into pocket editions,
tarnishing with torchlight
and an expression
of missed opportunities

Veracity

I say from enclosure
                    our highlights
transpose themselves on others,
                          though we'd like
to think ourselves apart
in Michael's valley,
a mote in the eye of the poet.
                      Settlement
voices up-the-ante, journalese
and typefaces, praise and rejection,
up-started in decomposing syntax:
I last loved then,
as unlike now.
Come now new chums, old hands,
dab dressers and company clones,
                      come gather
'round our table. In fits and starts
their lives apart altered facially,
configuratively. Age conflates
heritage with history, and most places
we step have been trod flat,
                    implicated
stress in a rhythm of here and there,
now and then,
in a snap,
re-aligned and made good
                  on the track,
a rival's masterpiece.

{ }
for Horst Ruthrof

excellent and skilled games slice
the skin that makes them temporal
time-systemed and terra-flopped,
as dedicated baselines read
to a packed amphitheatre—sollicitatio—and you know
how good the acoustics are
    in there,
intensely gradual, summum bonum
corporeal, corradiate in the guest-host
relationship, and a bit of goss
goes a long way over a cup of hot tea:
ah, deixas and modular furnishings
as if the terra-cotta were merely
a load of laminated table tops,
to spill, upon which, and other:
fragments of Fregean ex-
otica,

The Mouth Ulcer or An Ode To Subordinate Clauses

The slick suppuration that eyetooths
against the paint that hollows-out
the fleshy cavity and alters the pitch,
as if the instrument were out of tune;
praxis, the cruel theatre, the macabre
and salivating mouth that floats
like a children's programme
against the glowing backdrop
which is really black, unlike madness
which is purely and utterly an excess
of light or the over-enthusiastic packaging
of many small parcels of brilliance:
mouths are stuck through being discursive
or at least in part, their participation
implied if not pursued, or exe-cuted,
but this is chomping at the bit: anti-auto
this oral history, stuck as tetanus
against the rusty braces that brought
gossip on his rearing: boys at that
school wore no braces and nor did I;
ah, this archia, erasure in the fellated place,
as mouths crunch economics and ipseity,
as against sustain the lip-synch
strains the rhythm, squirrel-mouthed
she complains of big decisions
broadcast with no care for punctuation:
the ulcerate typo lost to endstop
or an unstuck glottal stop risen up,
necrotic on the mucoid surface.

The Dome of Saint Paul's Cathedral

emanates within the evening's
dark glow, fusing the spiritual mass
with a secular increase in power usage:
city lights needle like economic indicators
while the Thames thickens; an aging rock band—
stock epithet of the nineties—floats
drunkenly towards a sea
dark with heavy metals;
the millennium mushroom
plumes up and over and pigeons
seem like wrens in the appalling light

Erratum/Frame(d)

"Avant-garde texts evolve within a system of representation that is exclusively corporeal, natural, or borrowed from idealist philosophy. The thetic moment of rejection invests that system in an a-social present and keeps it locked there. The text therefore signifies an experience of heterogeneous contradiction rather than a practice, which, by contrast is always social."

Revolution in Poetic Language, JULIA KRISTEVA

"In judging the general outlay, it is always useful to have more than one manuscript of the writer, as he may have had to compress and fit his writing into too narrow a space like a small card owing to a shortage of paper, etc. and therefore to adjust his writing in a special case to unusual technical circumstances."

A Manual Of Graphology, ERIC SINGER

"Prior to the pattern of settlement then, which
is the passing flocks fixed into wherever
       they happened to stop,
the spirit demanded the orphic metaphor"

Aristeas, In Seven Years, J. H. PRYNNE

"The importance of language centered writing—all writing of diminished referentiality—is the writing and reading per se, as productional values (the writing as a production of production; the reading as a production of the text). Both writing and reading of these texts are aspects of a language production. What publishing achieves is an extension of circulation on the basis of exchangeability. The act of publishing always runs the risk of producing an occultation of a use value by an exchange value."

From The Notebooks, STEVE McCAFFERY

Prologue

The I undoes the field
& no means of exchange
takes place & nothing can be
determined as history
as records aren't kept
& there are no distinguishing
filial marks to barter

after a period of residence
mishap in cross tabulation
un-ranges the identified surface:
the page officially folds
& collected data makes categories
outside the mother tongue

LANGUAGE SHIFT CENSUS

the dialect as identity
tosses its hand into the ring
like a pagan mythology
they claim as outsiders
step in & bargain with strange
goods. the maintenance of lingo-
ecology as per strategies
in the dissolution of picaresque,
glottal & volta in second generation
shifts, the reeling transference

exchange by recognition
the official & major language
ratified by familiar expression:

Language Shift Census

matrix: the place
& outlook outside
the period of residence:
distribution of marginal
passages, attrition,
reversion, & the actual
of, the high or low numbers
that graph trends
shared as speech
in linguistic

Erratum

Every link (is) a separation.

    "and this the
floodloam, the deposit, borrowed for
the removal. Call it inland, his
nose filled with steam & his brief cries."
J H Prynne, "Aristeas, in Seven Years".

panchromatics: testy sundial
intersecting a bright array
less necessary (non-plussed) than
sight or loss as pages
help selves confer centre-
pieces like a jigged inward
road they've long since [lost]

fineprint in silent over-
tones, trast gnomic & heuristic godpath
loves still as all is well
& goodly politics dwell as audit
(tory) truth allusively: sand-$s
& expeditions as dead in deader trees

the river's swerve as oft is shored
against the surfaced strain,
in cleft & vein, text urs a looping
range, we cross the bridge in iron sur-
rounds, opaline a compass'
s doom, popular & pyritic the dry bed turns

?: light gives what, directs as form,
sinecure or set the leafy frame: time not been
in lisping ana-strains: red dust stuffs the pans
& boats are nothing short of crazed:
stuck as the bloody compass!

tributary empire gutted as imperial
craft bad taste the furthest flung & busy
cases: ratio (that diatribe) hook across
the watershed & laugh the ebb
of ancient language: I innate Le langage, cet
inconnu, & respect no prop
or stolen nouns: the charts re(ad) up-
side down

links as loose as solvent[s-at] parties
Azev-vous une piece d'identité: violent/
corri(gend)um via the surgical scan-
ning, subterfuge & malicious group
ing of words, space left as calmatives:
rare species of birds drinking (only) sand

riparian la high water marks a Southron accent
against the loving policy: crush not the
equal body or holy-weighted equi
librium, all tenure & scud, the combing showers.

dunes do fume, the poet said, sidecut mainsails a-bolting
kedge, the graphs or frame hard spoken, oilskins
dredging the babbled pentecost as speech pre & post
binds the universal congregation:

inner, time to collect the hay as bales
pyro black in plastic (what should) be a brilliant day, the soil
as clean as water locked away
impedimenta & hush hush against the hol-
low rock, dieresis(tic) tic tic the foäm as red
as sheets of slough &
long-range drought

drag-hooked again
the quasi-structures,
skim the typos, cadenza,
river's slipshod
utterings

anticlines: halus and kasar

piercing salt domes
pilot wells spring
commercial prospects
rise in fields given
more than a coded
number come oil tapped
in the basin, but no
anticline: occurs
only on a surface
though less so
when the camp
is dry and
entertainment
comes mail order
from Canberra

Every now & again thoughts of Bombay enter the heads of those in Bangalore

pre-dawn road-sulking in the garden city
some strolling or waking up or perishing in Cubbon Park—
why go elsewhere(?)—Chaturvedi Badrinath
of *The Times* [printed in Bombay] says the foundation
of human freedom & night in Dharma & Jainism
are radically different from those
that are provided in the western political
& legal philosophy of modern times.>this place
is pure(ly) structure's lists of the unbuilt & un-
finished like languages evolving
with social predicaments so new stories are added
well & truly lived in
satellite dishes like cribs of images
beggar bowls aimed to heaven—
becoming clearer
they neglect groundswell(s)
of opportunity (in Bombay
the stock-exchange is thriving!)
as Ta Ta trucks ARE their own trend
passing luminescent (but) smog-washed[?] BUT glowing
boulevards of optimism, the script
as clichéd as eucalypts
around Bangalore University—fluoro tubes
& whitewash & Hamlet prowling
or maybe skulking in the heat, dark eagles
shadowed Möbius against the skyline

while below, stealth moves with dogs, pigeons, parrots,
sparrows, rats & a white-tipped wingéd creature
that circle images of Ganesh, olfactory & sensing
every crow-movement, scent[ed] offering of orange
white & yellow flowers
piled high & illuminating all roadside temples
betwixt neo-dravidian state legislature
discouraging beggars but not tourists

who take more & unwittingly drink tap water
from branded bottles

What with the mass exodus of
models to the land of milk and
money, local choreographers weep
with frustration at the thought of
their carefully nurtured beauties
only working with the likes of
Hemant Trivedi and Lubna Adams.
Well, given the general standard of
the local-yokels, who'd want to work
here anyway? Especially when you
think of the pittances the poor
models get paid, compared to what
they earn in Bombay. Well, the
choreographers only have themsel-
ves to blame, for in their desperation
to get work, they quote the most
ridiculous of rates to their local-
yokel clients and then force the local
models to perform in abysmal
shows a staff reporter for
Bangalore This Fortnight writes
with a fit of pique

warnings over handling
corpses which may harbour
disease appear as lit. theory
on the walls of bookshops
while crickets chirrup so loud
the trees hum like circulars in the state
library in Kidney City as organs
are quickly put on ice for transfer
into richer bodies but this

IS poverty just like splendid saris
near the aquarium which promotes
fish as brain food
& the first jet made in India
shooting frozen flames on a muggy day
as somebody reads that <in his messianic drive
against eunuchs, pimps, brothels and gambling dens,
Mr Navalkar would often don garbs & disguises,
even wearing an afro wig on one occasion to gather
information on Bombay's sexual habits> while
nearby Vidhana Soudha in neo-dravidian
[state secretarial & legislature], unlocks a cabinet door
of pure sandalwood, carves art as policy
& repeats the pandora's box of campaign victories—
at least in the memories of the seasoned legislators,
& Attura Kacheri with new Corinth-ian-
esque columns poured in concrete &
Visvewaraiah Industrial & Technological
museum & Venkatappa Art Gallery &
glam houses & crystal palaces & Parsi Fire Temple
& Ganapati Temple & Sampangi Rama Temple
& St Marks & St Marys are noted by
the traveler in the all-day-hire taxi
moving through Bangalore like the slow evacuation
of congestion while at the dravidian
bull temple by Kempa Gowada, the
bull wandering & consuming all groundnuts
despite resistance appeased only by the temple
& a celebration
of the victory of ART like divining
& astrology (it reveals, Tantra relieves) & predicting earthquakes
& the Nehru Planetarium
& the green waters of Ulsoor Lake
& the Maharaji's imitation Windsor Castle
& banyan trees, neem & flame trees, chikakai tree

[85]

that ground down keeps the hair clean
like the mynah bird knowing who it was
that killed Laura Palmer
while Kempe Gowder 1 made Ulsoor
to store drinking water for his troops

& Dom Moraes reads between the tenses
in Bombay: "The lonely traveler is warned
            That ours is not a safe territory
                Since Rictus from the cave returned"

Across the road from the hotel a line is forming outside the gates
of the Galaxy Cinema. The billboard glowers Hum Apke Hain
Koun! A man & a woman. The man in braces & a white linen shirt
leans out of the frame & looks determinedly up to my fourth floor
window. He knows me. The woman leers at him. The line of
cinema goers recognize the conniving wife in her. This is a film
about power. Her sari is orange & silk & suggests Bombay liberalism. The
            bamboo
scaffolding (festooned?) with crows is about to collapse. It is an old
cinema. Eagles circling overhead are zinc-grey, dust brown
& as money changes hands
there is closure.

Self-Portrait Without Glasses

1

I am outside
& the rain
has blown the rusty
guttering
doused the fig tree,
porch light ghosting
squat concrete
columns
that would make
this porch different—
architects specializing
in duplexes are conscious
of things like this,
even in low-income
areas—familiar
as I am
with these
surroundings
I remove my glasses
& re-interpret—the squat
becomes a lazy streak
condensing
minus
five dioptre—a squint
that will not focalize
Corinthian
or lay at length
the Waldeck Nursery
monotony

2

A chilli merges
with the glowing tip
of a skywriting
cigarette—trans
firefly or lip slippage
premeditating
a meteorite fizzing
down thru the outer
atmosphere.

Landscapes
merge
& concepts
associate
with blocks
of colour.

Floodlit in an open window
& "you'll catch
your death": the sound
isn't heightened
but there are variables
of light.

3

Roadkill & G-locking:
I stagger amongst cars
streaming the highway's
Möbius strip:
crime qua crime
but not in full possession
of the facts
I feel compelled to drop
the case: good sight
IS intransigent,
despite the forecaster's
radar-echoes
scripted as paling & palsy
cops too pissed
to give evidence
after a record
bust.

4

I sense too a neighbour
wondering about rain & shadow
only Frankenthaler could
with confidence instil
rooms as inking puddles
& without my glasses
I might shuffle forward
& fall—like my son
who says that television
shows lolly-bloated children
sinking through the floor.

Poem As A Room

They don't pick up phenomena
with their x-ray machines & scanners,
and frisking simply presses
the point. Fragments of my

body's electrical vari-
ations and pent up energies
all potentially quantum and just
looking for the gap to infil-

trate. Anyway, the bulk of them are
here, in this room at the Royal
Hotel, where sunlight invests its un-
seen colours, the sky is not blue

and but for taste a cherry will
look like a swollen blueberry,
and an absence of love will become
a lifetime's passionate affair.

I guess things here are like this because
of (an) interaction between
the necessity of phenomena
and the unique properties of

this room. My enthusiasm
for breaking down the boundaries
between the actual and potent-
ial comes with this poem, this room.

A (C)ode for Simon Templar

"He's having so much fun
speaking code
But he can't tell you
what it's for—"
THE CELIBATE RIFLES, *Les Fusiles Celibataires*

"The weather is syntax
Thus we can speak of a cold of poetry"
LYN HEJINIAN, *Oxota*

A strange cold blew out
of distress, and sleep ignored you: good thing

it was then and only then (I)
turned up: my long neglected

country house full of obje(c)t d'
art and tasteless—comes of absence

and my housekeeper calling (sic).
Gets right to the bones, this diamond

frost like razor wire, a trap sprung
from inside like all good/proper

sex, which is me-mory; shall we?
They might call this the Russian way:

negating and coming down though
I like your kid gloves anyway—

or am I just moving my lips,
you Americans like it both

ways plus, as for myself a bouquet
of roses, no, maybe (only) three:

yellow for friendship, pink for love,
and red for lust, no, make that passion.

Hey, this just doesn't sound familiar,
unless hanging out at Bondi

has rendered me
useless in the eyes of polite

society, but Christ, did I
lord it over those Aussies:

my alabaster skin, halo
of antimony, snappy

dress sense, ability to make
clever jokes about Marx, Mao and Ché.

Beyond W. Eugene's Photographic Essay: "Life Without Germs" (*Life*, September 26, 1949)

A research facility called "Lobund" shrouded
in a night we guess is perpetual, the architecture
crematory, though not incendiary—a dark foreboding rot-
down may spark, fill the chamber, and catch the suited alien
unawares, a representative of the human species
seeking to penetrate the mystery behind the thickened glass.

A Bela Lugosi leer, and not before time, the glass
eye of the microscope masking the light source, the shrouded
cell budding or mutating or both: foetus of a contrived species
devastated by routine conjecture, the shattered architecture
of its pre-life fed like the lay photographer or the alien
with whatever information they've got to spare; whatever rot.

Flesh absorbs in the harsh light, the residue or rot
of an experiment (a success we should gather), the glass
of the test-tube marked by the tip of a nail, the control alien
in its purity, though over-exposure deceives: shrouded,
the truth lies packed in trays of the just-born, an architecture
absorbed by that of the chamber, by the decreation of a species.

Compare the moral beauty of the rat and the face of a species
hidden behind a suit and a mask, that of a monkey and the rot
filling creases of guilt sculpted from rubber, the architecture
of iron, wheel valves, and gaskets, the portholes of glass
constantly resisting face-presses from stiffly shrouded
creatures that reek of B-Grade Sci-Fi horror flicks: alien.

The hand that reaches into the core of its being is alien
to itself: in the House of Usher the monkey reclines, a species
separated though connected for the duration of its shrouded
life with data accumulated by its peers. Its veins may rot
but its eyes remain stoical if apprehensive, their glass
sheen more dignified than the eyeless rat's fallen architecture.

Before opening the envelope that speaks the architecture
of the surface must be exposed cleanly, a discovery is alien
and as such must be revealed within the clarity of glass
and not obscured by extras (hair, fur, flesh). The species
of germ observed, removed, stored, and labelled, the rot
of the host's body is discarded. Even the living are shrouded.

The architecture of body and tomb will vary between species,
whether germ, animal, or alien—it's a fact that rot
obscures experimental glass, that a world germ-free is shrouded.

harbour, god ode

harbour, aqua-
line green as
tide
plates & layers
fizzle stick py-
lons (tanged & butted
      like skull caps)
sagacious & divining
quorums of god
& good sea-sense

From Westminster Bridge: The Thames &:

bob & badmouth compatriots:
the prima facie distress
of canoes peeled by speedboats
& the vapours, crosses mere apparitions
on top of their spires, St Paul's
calling bells & imperfections
in the rhythms: ah, the tides
of faith! the brick & pewter
pebbled shores
almost polished, the edges
taken off & going easy
on the feet of scavengers,
who collect & should be thanked
as a grebe inspects the orbiting body
of an over-inflated balloon,
a sun destroying detritus,
the river's gravity
or a marginal star
sending out its last stream
of wavering light,
hoping for ascendance.

red sonnet & I

as the secret's out & lamely
I trace steps out of dust fine & distraught
on a perfect flat surface: body-
fabric stretched taut & breaking
down—a lapse like blood shot through
the wreck of an explorer's sailboat
left marooned on the rim
of an empty inland sea.
take it as red.
& dead the forms
at sunrise, nights
spent open under meteor
showers all ultra, & downputting
urban phobias. a red mist imagines nicely.

Visionary Dreariness

The poem, (de)void of association,
wallows in the metaphor it substitutes
for index, & in the contexture of canonization
forms extrinsically sublime renditions
(as reflex) on the bushland enclave

near the river's withered edge—Blackwall Reach
& its limestone cliffs compacted granular
though still aery & breathing
with the mechanical distinction

that allows concrete yachts to float,
the houses on prime real-estate looking to the view
they perceive outsiders might suggest,
the fog rising over the extracted liminal corpses,

the tide's seaward retreat leaving water low
in the caves at the base unreachable except
by abseilers, swimmers, or mariners
defining each component part

of our investigation & hypothesis, the
need to paint our thoughts into speech:
that you'd rebuild on such abstractions
the failing seasons, the climate changing

& unpredictable & everything saline,
that despite the buttresses that guard
"your spot" or notions of exclusion
like pet words in-utero the whole thing

might be seen as the diminishing rec-
tangle of childhood, cast out the anglers
with their choking spools, sidereals
orbiting & hunting ellipses

just a matter of density when the scales
give an exact or precise answer
under a certain set of conditions,
winter coming & fork lightning

rendering class operable only
as abjection, the dormer windows filled
with suicides, expensive saloon cars sunk
subterranean in their ports like funeral craft

swallows all but darting through recesses
in half-lit solid rock, the sandspit washed
into the channel, mulloway stiff near
the shores in primitive accumulation —

transformation into newsprint or a brief article
in a fishing periodical, these comparatively
narrow stretches of water marked by
street names & monumental works

above catacombs reflecting a sub-tropical
culture too heavy for surfaces, alliterative
as the State lulls or loses the electorate,
as the owner of a boat weighed down by cormorants
senses it's just like you'd stood there before.

Velcro (R)

Velcro — horizontal

Velcro first came unstuck—no, ripped apart—dangling
modifiers the words were shining—like poems without

reference, the static shreds signifying all that around
which the rhetoric twines, not seen as tactile or imminent.

out there in the open air they velcroed up & took in the view,
denying all was machinery & mechanics in the hills incendiary

the sun with a sting warms things up as the flesh sings & is com-
fortable to be part of a tableaux that is poetic and still reads like prose.

the horizontal text of the fields on the far side of the faultline
denies the margins: the rough turf veritable underfoot, like

burrs gripping their lush socks: without reference they test hormones
on sheep, the wool peeled or plucked, each strand a morpheme juxt-

aposed on the table, in microns the growth sounds, all opposition
as buyers rival & the genetics of velcro is seen as a good thing:

con-text a sideshow at the ag. show as they can't find much common
ground, on the fine day sealed against the cold, they marvel privately.

in-refrain they would come together if the other changed but too
much would seem against it, the patented picaresque, the first draft

excluded though not by DE-sign, irritating living in each other's
pockets like a finger-nail on chalk-board breaking the camel's back

way out there beyond the faultline, where the centre becomes a brand-
name with exposure: if demand drops & the market fails rumours

become useless: a radar dish a rare geology deflecting the script, holus-
bolus on the intergalactic fringe & outside the eye nothing to do with

the body. It's not about synthetics, ours is a history of metal
& this is an aberration out here. Ours is as ours & the forges

are on the country's fringe, the belly-dumpers & haulpacks eating
the salt & forming guilds. a union of metal. & one of them says

Karl Shapiro might have said "Driven by tiny evils." or "And hands
as high as iron masts, I sleep" sealed in the southern hemisphere—a

dacron sleeping bag with velcro instead of a zipper, metal-less near
the intense theodolite positioned on the long highway devoid

of deviations, with the hawks all about at sunrise to make us feel nature-forged & outside denials, transliterated as tympanizing stele.

such we are rejected & compose as repetition the variation on a patented item that is quite adequate, always closing our teeth on the soil.

VELCRO — VERTICAL

Sharply, serrated and
unsettled all chalk and nails
on the absorbent blackboard
smug and satisfied when set or sitting
back the grip and placement enjambed
or askew in closing the turned on
turned off static! Lip lip stuck
& left behind like frostbite
which we could imagine sounds
a lot like velcro   .
brutalized — yes, the bitter
price of absence bites
gnashed designated or left behind
in shadow or even under water   [by God knows who]
adhering security as breath
or breath as black as God
sealed beneath a reflecting surface
bound down beside the burred jacket
we left behind like skin
as bed clothes, moved together
as one AND so on: sparkies
stuck to overhead power —
lines across the page of course,
discourse or labelled quotes
on grey school socks and fighting

in the changerooms, even leg ropes
come the bitter
wipe-
out
lauded over who or whom receives
a technical pleasure (unstuck AS mis-
begotten the tarnished fabric spoken
 holding hips worn
with constant rip and closing, a soft end un
and unable to take or take hold: Yes,
let's close the TOTal gap
and move a-part only part-ially
as gesture: static and the carpet &
the exclamAtion, which like silicon chips
and cats' eyes set in asphalt
is politically)

* * * * * * * *

The velcro river
making sure no crazy boats
go wide against the dis-tant   COURSE
banks, no logic in the sweeping curve
or letting loose close to the mouth
which we've prove(d) as speech: a delineation
of the body search & picaresque
where colour is style & sound
THE ergonomics, river body
loaded and magnetic, rocky outcrops
ampersands in style and would-be
movement/s—all that heat
and waterless space hanging over
like a backdrop   [Basil Bunting
obsessive   manipulated
& needing fo-   Into place the

[105]

cus, which in multi
and A con served
no less as spirit, picaresque
says source, I love it!
knows

"It was not so,
  scratched on black
   by God knows who,
    by God, by God
      who.]

* * *

adheres in stratas
the velvet sheets of flesh
or water, the hooks
of anglers tagging
the river's debris

* * * *

attracted singularly
though in endless strips,
intersecting sibilance
when they try to quietly
remove their velcrosed feet
to keep clean sheets (crisp)

* * * *

Soil & ground cover
all exclusions, they expect
it back.

& the sound it makes
when parted: a moist rip
that counts the hours
before the strips of our bodies
are layered back
in place.

[106]

*der(i)vation

is the sleep we tell
you I or you I told
i.e. we told
& had to have
to make it happen
over

*deception

is not sleep
but sleep not had
a derivation
in deprivation, meant only
as
endear-
ment. Meant!
rest-ful!

*de-pri-vation

the body vegetable
& sun-reliant
de (i) fies
silent & silence
a mov(i) e parting, cut & dried
black & white, no current
or late(nt) magnetism
going to put it on track,
no back to look:

sleep and slept
in-ept & peeping out of lack
which could be seen
as a kind of threat,
a part(icularly) vicious
interpretation of something mellow,
like a softcore Rothko
not hung like breath
but watching as the sea
is its own decor,
rates the hands
are e(s)sential: no de Sade could understand though he might
the interwoven hair
but red
& sees in and through sleep as breath
stained sanguine despite the translucence
of decision resolution,
hope as gest-
URE!

SHarply woke(n).
their habits more convenient
with the intro-
duction of velcro: prayers
stick

VELCRO (R)

the body osmotic
almost symbiotic
& cumulative:
the left & right
sides of movement

thought
& co-ordination
as a separate issue: this
translation
interp (re: tation &)
practic/se & a stroke
bringing back the French
he'd not spoken for forty
years, he could not
speak (in) English or revert
to clean sailing the hooks
of commodity fetishism
straightened become prongs
in a bed of language's
disciplinary
general-iz-
ation or instinct or the wealth
of our post-colonial lust
for deference & discipline
justifying only in familiar speech
lacking (all) ident-i-
fication, the sky outside
the/his recovering window
blue velvet, velvet blue
the river flows

traduction
interp (ré: tation &)
pratique(r) & une attaque
ramenant le français
qu'il ne parlait plus depuis quarante
ans, il n'a pas pu
parler (en) français ni retourner
au ça-plane-pour-moi les crocs
du fétichisme du produit
redressés deviennent des clous
dans un lit de la
général-is-
ation disciplinaire du langage
ou l'instinct ou la richesse
de notre désir post-colonial
de la déférence & la discipline
justifiant seul dans le discours familier
qui manque (toute) ident-i-
fication, le ciel en dehors
de la/de sa fenêtre récupérante
velours bleu, bleu velours
le fleuve coule

Night Seeding & Notions of Property

Dizzy with figure-eighting
the corners of his fields, the drills
filled with seed & super

& closed over under
the tattooed rash of night,
foxes' muffling barks

& fighting to cover tracks
with a starpicket the axis
of a compass whose North

is wire-guided & lethal: silver
tennis balls exploding in their spiralled
swing on totem-tennis poles

for here stillness shivers & moves
like frost moves the shattered
flesh of quartz

over the wasted plots. A clear
dawn is soluble anyway
& the tractor gnaws,

its queasy stomach
turning slowly & coldly
with winter:

                    dispossessed
the farmer moans—a sudden downpour
shaves his precious topsoil.

The ghosts clamour about the microwave
& television set, the stove broods
in this sauna of politeness.

City people are expecting billy tea
& damper & the sheep to bleat
in unison. Nous regrettons parler.

There wasn't a kangaroo to be seen.
Night-seeding, the tractor's floodlights
are blood-red & ovarian —

nurturing the cloddish soil, & always
the farmer working the wheel, hands
gnarled & frostbitten & large.

Ornithology

(I)

They set out before dawn with optical instruments
pens and notebook. By the lake they will create
poems without reference. This refuge in the suburbs
covered in mist like a smokescreen, the traffic nearby

moving to and from another front. Night herons
will be making their way to daytime roosts
while vast flocks of cormorants and ibises
will be shaking the droplets of night moisture

from their wings. Ripple-flex will break the lake
with the first dives of a darter, serpent high-headed
on a technical neck. The sun's appearance will subvert
the abject waters. [Rhythm is shock as all erupts.]

(II)

One observer whispers *cacophony*, the others say
don't interrupt. It cannot be determined who joins in on
this riposte, so none can be quoted. The birds are prosy
one might suggest but translation is tyranny—

traduire, c'est trahir, referring to crib notes as per habit
and (migratory tendency). An odd bird lifts blithely and they
simultaneously gesture, forgetting birds or explanations
or flight. *This bird developed of itself in isolation?*

the Russian ornithologist asks. *Its call is beyond our own*,
his Australian hosts reply. He seems satisfied and takes note.
Under the heading "Ostranenie" he writes: a night
heron awakening with sunrise, and going about its

swamp-stalking business in full light, weight of the old world
on its shoulders, threatening closure, drip-dry feathers
coming unstuck and tilting disdainfully contrary, rejecting
camouflage in the roots of tea-tree and paperbarks, denying

its geography, blurring genre. That this should happen diurnally
does not spoil the observation. These binoculars being *trained
to look where they shouldn't* in this upside-down climate.

Skeleton weed / generative grammar

(I) FINITE-STATE

The "i" takes in what is said—
yes, it is easily led
across the floors of discourse
only to find itself a force
easily reckoned with: there's
no point in stock-taking arrears
as fleshly interests tell you
nothing except acceptability & taboo.
Take skeleton weed infesting
the crop—rosette of basal
leaves unleashing a fatal
stem with *daisy-like* flowers
that drop (into) parachute clusters
of seeds. One missed when
they scour the field (men
& women anonymously-clothed
seated on a spidery raft dragged
behind a plodding tractor,
monotony testing the free-will factor),
can lead to disaster.

(II) PHRASE-STRUCTURE

{[((analyz)ing)] [the ((constituent)s)]}
we examine(?) the wool of sheep
for free-loading skeleton-weed seeds,
their teeth specifically designed
for wool: the ag department
have decided they ARE selective
though admit our investigations
will help their "research".

(III) TRANSFORMATIONAL

One year the farmer asked us if we
felt guilty for missing one & hence ruining
his would-have-been bumper crop.
Quarantined the following year. Losing
his unseeded would-be bumper crop.
Ruining his credit rating. His marriage.
His son's & daughter's places
at their exclusive city boarding
schools. His problem with alcohol.
His subsequent breakdown
& hospitalization. (?) We remained
& still remain passive. We still remain
& remained passive. Still we remained
& remain passive. But we [look(ed)] deeply,
collectively & independently
into our SELVES. Our silence
was an utterance of a loud inner speech.
A loud inner speech was an utterance
of our silence. Speaking for myself,
I've included in my lexicon of guilt
the following: what I feel today
will I feel tomorrow? And those tight
yellow flowers: so beautiful on the wiry
structures they call "skeleton weed".

Ruse

—a poem beginning & ending with lines by Edwin Denby

Real disaster
is
so near   us
a ruse albeit
in the vein
of [white] lies
still not only
poor taste
but i-
(m)moral: I see my hand screwed up
             through an auger's throat,
             twisted & spat-out, that auger
             humping its load all the way
             to the pile, diesel
             coughing its guts in limp
             balls of exhaust-ion: body
             fluids decorative as a hawk
             tracks field mice zigzagging
             through gold-red grain
             stockpiled & illuminated
             eye-sky-wise.

UR-US

for Lyn Hejinian

Dis-trust close company
wherein the should of words
nudges the courtesies
best displayed in public,
like reading palimpsest
as
object, the mirrored growth
ethnographic though distant,
we close distraction
as sounds in high-strung
webs of branches, eerie
deliberation (as)
black-shouldered kites
per-sist,

spilling too large but neat
in bravura
& rolling slightly over(tly)
the repetitious fields
undulating like gutturals
burnt in much-frequented loss,
the rippling burns of & up the wind-
rows

as (in) the loss fauna gains re: the sign
coinciding as dead bones themselves
contentiously
AGAINST the historic heap

that I take lines best used by a more
affection -ate date: this thin frame
might less inform its sex,
as naked the ghosted hands
still linger, smoothing the sharp bumps

or ribs in primary
numbers

you alone are IT
as target, though not enough the UNpolitical
failure that might de-note
the solitary
in the uniquely injured crow whitely
starking the sky, interned the crops,
the grains of its ergotic eyes
as ripening these potential caw
caw caws against speculation
when the group owns
the single farmer's wheat. No, it
is us with whom they have their beef? or
delicate—too—the pericardium
that protects nothing but
sacks of blood, 16 to the acre, but we as us
are tougher than they think & will ride side-saddle
to the buckling tray of the pick-up, the contorted air-
tunnels of the Royal Fly-ing Doctor
come flow-ing up from Carnarvon.

I need no boundaries yet
need
ask per-mission
to climb the Needlings,
no longer part
of (A) family land de-
spite a maiden Aunt surfing the house-split
as Meckering quaked & an epi-centre
halved the distance
between dreams & gout

or ever-lasting
dried as drought
& gulleys open (ed/ing) their archaeologies
for evidence: the Nyoongah stookers
re-&-re-&-re-curringly re-mind family
of dis-possession
as time in a dark light
best not gone out in
but waiting against the crazy predictables
that might leave the weather
for stooks or bone-shaped will-o-the-wisps
a threat that should ENRICH the land
like mimic & eyes eaten when looked
too close;

      ah, as us I buffer enclaves
& camouflage against the bow-waves,
the plough covering the tractor's
heavy diurnals, lambasting clay-clods
ripped in a welter & tossed into a kind-of
scummy order

but no signature, lest it be the way
they close the corners,
always
the figure-eights
cry for order
as the quail or plover
rise staccato in their manic
helicoptered flights
& in frost après-ski
in a way that singularly we'd never net
re-spect, to(gether) form a loose (but)

intere-
sting
team
& all periphery watch in
heavily wintered/sun burnt.

longevity is the length
of a solitary word
lift-
ed from its con-
text & freed

they opened the aviaries & the birds native
to the place returned to perish on the wire netting
during their long vocational absence from the parish

(those) introduced were seen at random or heard in &
out the years, as place, as no sign the damage, and all male, hybrid

they wrote in lemon ink
& later held it to the light
to ensure the words (in) visible
on blank whites
w[h]ere reaLLy & should they be
sum-mon(ed).

trace elements, rise & fall soil affecting Us
as
      acid, a need for burning & acrid sweet the dousing rays
of kero, replete & choking as

applicator

this loaded contrapunctual glory
maisonette in which politely we only pre
the tend (ency) as hearing should, whisper
as heavy as
clod crushing rollers
anvil or injected chop-
ping blocks, iron-headed shatter
that begs sculpture or firewood:
sidereal periods ro-
tating against the sullen
sparks

?: or the luminous flux ala
candela, no, that IS agisting
reason, & should we have
some of that, the luminous INtent
sity of the young girl closing
curtains in & of a deeply south-
ern lighthouse, or lux
(SI — ILLUMINANCE) as I see lens-crack
anyway & spirit an eye-deep illusion
in clarity & consistency, here I see for all of us
& you must trust me: sunlight hard & cold
& referencing against stock epithets
we KNOW(n) as poetry,
the girl in her highboots collecting
sentinel curs at the base of our psyche,
imposed against the weathered
blemish. parrots fly north & carry
psittacosis that affects their speech. West west west
they rumour, that soggy linchpin de-
fining centuries, against the wrecks.

ah, the quotas & post-ing the
bans, so short in breath
& pillars of & as car-
yatids keeping us
apart

Graphing The Tremors Of Narrative

a second poem for Lyn Hejinian

*

most tremors go undetected other than on seismographic
      equipment
the tremors of speech hesitate, the glottal stop drops beyond
      comparatives:
the ruptured narrative sheers the palate & compresses the tongue's
      surface.

*

in the tremor, sound-byte
on graph-paper she writes each letter
to a double millimetre at all angles
the word-plates shifting: words don't tolerate
unless through redefining surface. i.e. the epicentre
lies above the focus & you editing a (recorded)
disaster: word-cutting with tape as hyphen
& this the system. Patronizing, this capturing
of folksy rhythms out in the country, or at the academy
with Ivor Winters & his "dogma that once material
becomes words it is its own best form" for Blackmur's
      nothin' on Frost &
that's the rub (*langue & parole*)! cutting a word kills
the need for hyphen, & each square within the page's
definition doubles up as tool or meaning: measuring our intention,
our need for language. in the splicing we track down slowly
perfect point which as it happens will be exact: that in-breath
murmur taking over & you can't even tell it's not how
you'd spoken or might in future or given the chance again
choose to speak: the in-breath taking over as you illustrate—
the hungry gunman who'll stop at nothing or tattoo guns
never stopping—*that* keeps the ritual going (a tin-shack
on the city's outskirts, the tremors not even leading
to a jump in syntax & the sentence holding up despite
by-laws—the possessive [which is not the object] objecting,
the subject escaping before the ground opens up in full
sense-around & swallows): on the faultline the guttural

[123]

sounds are mesmeric: the internal dialogue of structures,
the stone columns that hold the surface between utopias.
the magnet is metonymic, though tremors in the field
must be metaphoric. the gunman might shoot you
& you being there coincidentally at the time might simply
be substitution for a victim that should be the one who refuses
to hand across the money without a fuss, whereas you're
just out to do the shopping or looking dreamily into the window
at something that's taken your fancy. "your" being there is symbolic.
though the media don't speak in metaphors. they need contexture.
the tremors of your dislocated day flow this way *with*
                    fluidity & resonance.
the fragments of the shattered city (gunshot breaks
the glass) retain form when (re-) built on graph paper.

each editor has a language to describe the processes of their work.
each tremor is a fragment of production, the re-shaping of an
                    utterance. if you read
the nineteen eleven edition of Britannica the Thylacine is not
extinct nor would its editors without knowing the characters
of Tasmanians have guessed that within twenty five years
it would be "it once" or "was": the tense changes within the
                    narrative. ad infinitum.
Yes, I would also like to wonder from which home Patty Hearst
was snatched but cannot pre- or suggest the narrative. the words
hang on the graph's fault lines: within the walk from Wheatlands
to Needlings there are infinite points of potent(ial) stop-over
though we can't stop at all of them. let's highlight splits
in the land, points where the '69 quake broke free its focus
& snaked out through the wastelands, shattering salt growths,
sending showers of hot crystals towards the clouds like luminous
rain, forming gulleys along the path of rupture. these gulleys
                    the burst veins
of all that get in the way of the gunman as he ties
the disparate fragments of *the* poem together.

as I sell out to your voice & your voice only an electrical storm
suggests there is a link between all natural phenomena. that we
scrutinize the essence of this & label our acceptance of disaster
as *a priori*. I knew before you this storm-over-the-river
would strike hard & be less specific—you can't guess where
the next fork will strike but certain places are more likely—
conductors are impatient & will attract our attention, just as
goading that gunman will take a future scene to the casualty
     room
           or cemetery. indulgent
this graph as it twists on the drums. that you said
     graphologically
"I perceive the world as vast & overwhelming", somewhere
cadavers {our gunmen's victims} will give-up their organs
         like libations, the hands
that take them struck tremulous, removed in sequence.

Placebo

—a third poem for Lyn Hejinian

> *"Save me, O God; for the waters are come into my soul."*
> PSALM 69.

> *"homines quoque si taceant, vocem invenient libri"*
> Inscr. Guilferbylanae Bibliothecae extracted from
> Steve McCaffery's PANOPTICON

Evening approaches & reflection:
how water so cool cuts through salt
after such a long dry spell. York cemetery
dusty & doves & hands & vandals or small burrowing animals
getting under the tombs—we walk amongst iron flowers
      collectively
denominations of iron flowers—though all souls are out
& looking in at we the warders guarding our [tense] hearts: yeh,
the Roundhouse in Fremantle would have suited Bentham
& you tell me Steve McCaffery is a quiet & intense man
who seethes with ideas. the placebo here is the notion of death
as we speak with each other's tongue, our accents so different.
Those sinking mounds where bodies have left bones behind.
fluffy animals in jars. clusters of ceramic flowers under glass
domes, finite universes.

THE ORDER FOR THE BURIAL OF THE DEAD:

*Here is to be noted, that the Office ensuing is not to be used for any
that die unbaptized, or excommunicate, or have laid violent hands
      upon themselves.*
*Vandals disguised as priests have broken angels. we attempt to
      rebuild them but settle on laying
their body parts in what we assume to be the right positions—a wing
grounded like a winged senegal dove or parrot struck by a car
      thundering through the country.*

[the cemetery is a grid]

SHOULD WE WORSHIP THE DEAD?

All around the paddocks are charcoaled, the burn-back ashing
          the soil; oxygen ripped
from the stubble's follicles, everywhere the offerings: as fire
rolled across the firebreaks it cremated wooden crosses—the
          unbaptised, the suicides
buried on the fringes.
          poetry looks out from consecrated ground &
          names the indifferent pink & grey galah
          as poet—it clusters with its familiars
          on the hot asphalt, collecting
          pre-noon shadows
inward the slabs collapse
too heavy to maintain
the stress, the fate
of all anthologies

the water-table rises bringing salt & corpse-rot to the surface
while families from Scotland recall their ancestors watching
over the graves of their loved ones to prevent body snatchers
plundering organs for wealthy natural philosophers
& you tell them how as a child you'd fill U-tubes
with ionizing solutions & place dead insects
in the crook of the apparatus & pass an electrical
charge through it believing it would restore life
to the corpses

[127]

the cemetery is the axis that keeps
the surrounding farms
in place

"learning
a certain geometry
of purely decorative shapes"
out there you wade through crypt-like salt crests
waiting for the tide to turn & catch you out—
here you can drown under the painful ore
of blue sky, seared & sun bleached:
"out there in the sun it's bloody suicide"
the old timers tell you
as shapes are shifted over the landscape's
decorative motif. They add cryptically
that feral cats hunt rodents
& drag brilliant parrots
from dead trees
which sit sentinel
in the centre
of paddocks
for years—
collecting
the phrases
of bird calls;
in wet years
reminding that drought
might be just
around the corner;
providing
tenuous shade for sheep
in summer.

[128]

Starting With Delmore Schwartz's "The Self Unsatisfied Runs Everywhere" A Precursor To *Syzygy*

Prologue or precedents:

Speaks for itself? This bird or poem's
warped astrology. They rote & ate in cycles.

Migratory, seeking or rejecting exile.
Enough to hate an open road or rile security.

Subtle feather on the pier cuts through shoe to foot.
Splintered glass on asphalt as hot as coal cools.

Language's lynch mob searches your mouth & finds
consonants. The vowels are stored for pleasure.

Real people are birds—there is a definitive
pecking order ad-hoc(k)ed & ritualized for longevity.

A blue sky here is diffident & seasonal. Night
spills over & taints. We gulp the photochemical air.

And yes, the "self unsatisfied runs everywhere": catching
up & busting out & going on the record. De-

pleting godheads & energy stocks. The heart trumped
& out there looking. The floor of the city close at hand.

Liaisons exotic & pouting under the steamy glass
of the Conservatorium, the hot fans blowing

an oozy melody. The shrill of the finespray sprinklers
relieving nought. You break-away & avoid collusion.

Out there it's cold & that's enough to beckon.
Or trigger a split in the personalities of gulls

adorning the greens of public gardens, scavaging
amongst the scraps, outing discretion.

NARRATIVE:

Depressed on the city fringe, out-skirting
rum deals & facilitating decline: yeh,
looking further afield & gloating: from on-high
or peering up through the gloom into the steady
hardened sunlight. In the front bars dart
players threaten & you recall the rules
of natural selection, ducking for cover
behind two brothers who lost each other
ten years earlier, their unsatisfied selves
breaking out & forgetting the way back:
chance has brought them here & recognition
comes only in the way they hold their beers.
Electric trains hiss, the rolling stock
glittering on the expanding tracks.
So, you hitch a lift & tell the driver
to take you anywhere & he obliges. Now closer
to the city centre you seize opportunity
& take in a parade. A super model rolls
past in a white stretch limousine, her
credentials on display. You share a flagon
with a guy from the Pinjarra people
& regurgitate love. You tell him this
is a journey of the heart & he asks
you to leave. Okay, but you've already left
& your mind runs everywhere. Opus Dei,
frenetic & enthusiastic & lost.

Symbol:

The bottlebrush trees fencing
the city cemetery
drag stale blood from the corpses
into their wiry flowers
& glow
revitalizing
lustrous & oxygenated
despite the ashen
haze. Gulls here too
loiter
as I wait for you to leave
the suicide's funeral.
I die here too
& this is after.
A cold re-
collection
as the glass pyramid
of the Conservatorium
lures & melds
the different personalities
I project: I am pleasant
but distant, my lies
are careless—within,
palms & tropical
exotica
pout with water
& heat.
If this is sensual
the bottlebrush flowers
cadmium & deep
stiff in a chill wind,
drain & temporize.
The traffic
thickens.

SOFTLY THE SELF LIES BELOW THE BRAZEN SKY:

The screech of shadowmaw gulls in clusters
about a zodiac of garbage & joggers increase

their pace. A high speed car chase along the
riverfront with traffic lights compulsive

& rigid & crimson. Floodlights sudden
& anhydrous lift a curving ball (r & r),

office workers hunch towards the ferries
like overdressed refugees fleeing

the crowded nodal jetties. The breath
of self ropes a crowded image & seeks

a face like yours per desire. Nightcrowds
fizzing below the beautifully inflective

surface, as softly the self lies
beneath the brazen sky.

Syzygy re:prise

NEW MOON: WORKS & DAYS

the ye(a)r
demo (lish) 'd in chunks
& hunks & slices
shatter-foiling
or plain-ly tinkering
'cros[s]   the chapt-
ered tarmac! rumside
the bars & lop-
sided shadows, all out
of kil-
ter. <but> getting
bett/ter newer moon
tektite Australite skystone
down plan-
etarium, those o so very
"stones"
"from"   "heaven"
chaputz & guzzling coff–ee& wary   (i) LY
galloning mnemonic or quoram flow-n
of jargon's acrobats
dolling out red red & more
red & sophistry an-
chors the dishes
long overdue & all of those juices
running askew. on with the show.

Lets habit - u ˜ u - c:
dis-tribution & vegetationals
stars & cluster penny perfect
discs
levelled love (l) y? inkwells
& funnels capped the quick dark smog
of their bodies: trap-door

& alluring, the bower
bi-valve gasping muscular
& we ad-
apt, twig lines are wire
& the streets barely visible,
street lights extinguished.
triggering
the trip wires & tricked
thoroughly the safety net:
co-co-on-ed
& architectural. ˜strings
maybe struck, jazz-like
& impro-
viz-
ATIONAL! just that stray
filament sizzling under-foot
as the primaries sat ˜u˜
rate. buff & bisque & tofu
& weapon - [con] (tr) - ary
blue. & this the new.

SUNDIAL*

Fuzzy lo- gic
the tick of confidence
time in trick boxes
& gestural (l) Y in media res,
printed face perfect
be (LY)! the etch & rive(n)
hues in angular
bronze bowstring equatorial trying
avoidance in the ornament

[134]

All "y" offsetting perfect
the pole archaic or other
WISE? that, move - able: horizon
in declination construed
as artificial, & we trust
the shadow, the stick.
those slight variations
in the equation of time:
"stands sub dio in the marble air."
semaphore as lower coffin
in the submariner's word
critically blue
as lavatically: cold
temporal ampli-
tude. dread [nought!]
Nan-tucket & gonzo-slip-pery
rocks = gnomon, style,
in the garden, ap-
par   en-ts(olar)
        day.

WITTGENSTEIN: THE MEANING OF A WORD IS ITS USE IN LAN-
GAUGE/

that flap=plastic orange & that
rip-pil & blown out like
THAT
in the strobe & Möbius
attribute re-putes
had like peas shelled
& potatoes par-boiled
their skins tacky
on the lino floor.

res-anno-tate & olve in-meet
in 2nd floor of a not-s-o
{mod build ern ing} smog
si
bi
la
n
t
logic bombs out
& systemiZes de-
feat & that wr(et)ched orange strip of plastic
IS a yellow flystrip.
to the floor of the ocean
*spliced flying angels
trapped and swum out breathLESS & limp
Troude waking yawning zips
twisted & spent, quote.
cite-ech-o
the earth-movers
de-odour-izing   Leonard Bloomfield
rhetoric & single(s)   *Language*, 1933

Bars: reprise
& Protagoras's lying
as (form) truth
go down pat. phono-
tactically & pitched
in com-mercial allophonic
time! (Re-
member, he broke a glass while you broke a window

SKY e{x: x is veridian}
& puce. the ktch ktch ktch
of the bus. the shiff & shiver
of sails twi-

                                              lit.

Tarot

for Jacques Derrida

1

PHARMAKON: OR ANXIETY SHELTERING IN
THE CRYPT OF CLOUDS, EXPLORATION A
MAP OF THE BLOOD CANALS WITH BARELY
ENOUGH FLESH TO COVER YOUR HANDS
WHICH LOOK LIKE WINGS ONLY IN SIL-
HOUETTE, CONDEMNED IN THE GESTURE
AND TRANSLATING *PHAEDRUS*, THAT YOU
ARE HERE IS NOW RUMOUR, YOUR ILLUSION
NOT SUBSTANTIAL ENOUGH TO COME AT
MYTH, THAT YOU WOULD SPECULATE TO
REPLY INCISIVE, BOUND IN THE URBAN
SETTING, A STRANGE BIRD WITH A BRASS
BEAK PICKING AT YOUR SWOLLEN LIVER:
THE DESIRE TO LOVE OUTSIDE A FUTURE

2

OUR FINANCIAL LOVE IS DISTRIBUTED EVENLY THOUGH
OCCASIONALLY CAUGHT   IN TRAPS THAT CLOSE DOWN
THE LIGHT AND PRESERVE THE INCREASING ENERGY OF
OUR ESTATE, *LE MONDE*, THE WORD REGENERATING AS
ORIGINS LAPSE AND WE PRY APART INFLECTIONS,AC-
CENTS, APOTHEOSISTIC AND LOVING OUTSIDE A FRUSTRAT-
INGLY PASTORAL DISCOURSE AS GLAS, AS 100 CUBIC INCHES

3

A TRINITY OF COINS GOES AGAINST THE
DEPLETION OR APPROPRIATION OF LABOR,
AS WE ENHANCE ITS PRESTIGE AS
TRADITION, THRIVING ON THE CONTRA-
DICTIONS. I SAW IT ON THE HILL IS WHAT
HE SAID WHEN HE GOT HOME FOR SUPPER,
THE BISHOP OF DURHAM WATCHING THE
CATHEDRAL FRACTURE WITH LIGHTNING
FIRE, THE METAPHOR BUILDING FROM IN-
SIDE OUT, HIS LESSON NOT OF INTER-
JECTION BUT FREE WILL AS NARRATIVE,
DISPLACING THE PLUMB BOB TEXT DRAW-
ING ITS NEAT LINE FROM HEAVEN TO HELL:
ALLEGORICALLY DENOUNCING CONFESSION

4

LIKE JETTIES INTO RIVERS WHOSE CLARITY IS
ONLY SKIN DEEP YOU DON'T LOOK AT RE-
FLECTIONS — WATER A PHOTOSENSITIVE
PLATE TO THE BODY'S NEGATIVE IMPRESS-
ION TAKEN ONLY IN PLACES WHERE SUR-
FACE IMAGES COLLECT & CANCEL OUT LIKE
CUTTLEFISH DECOMPOSING LIKE POP CULT-
URE AS THEY VOYAGE AWAY FROM THE
OCEAN, NOSTALGICALLY SEPIA AT A TIME
WHEN GLOBAL WARMING MAKES NOTIONS
OF SEASONAL CHANGE IRRELEVANT, THEIR
PINK-LIPPED HULLS DECORATING BAS RE-
LIEF, PASSIVE & RECEPTIVE & ADDING
FERTILITY WITH ARCHIMEDEAN ATTITUDE

5

HERE CARVED INTO THE SURFACE IS
GLEANED LIKE PAYDIRT AND TEN QUID ON
THE GAMING TABLE, CONTRASTING
EXPERIENCE AS PRECONDITION & LUCK AS
YOU STUMBLE HEADLONG LIKE A FLOCK OF
MIGRATING BIRDS INTO A JET ENGINE HIGH
ABOVE PASTORAL COUNTRY YOU ARE
INTENSELY FAMILIAR WITH, IT BEING BAD
LUCK THAT THE CROPS FAILED SO MANY
YEARS RUNNING AND THE WELLS
TURNING SALT: THIS, THE LOGIC OF
REJECTION WE FIND IN SEARCHING FOR
THAT ALLUSIVE INFLECTION, THE BRASS
TURNING WITH THE INCLEMENT WEATHER

6

INVASION, EXPELLING THE PRODUCTS
OF OUR LABORS, OUR LUST FOR SURPLUS
WILL BRING A KIND OF FREEDOM? HIGH
HOPES EASILY CRUSHED. TEN QUID ON THE
TABLE, TRANSGRESSING TO BREAK IT UP
THOUGH IT'S NOT THE PAGE OF STAVES,
THERE'S NO ACTING AND THE DISSOLUTION
HAPPENS WITHOUT YOU NOTICING, UP-
TURNED LA MAISON DIEV IS ATMOSPHERIC
WITH RECEPTION BROKEN UP BY TONGUES
OF FIRE THE SPIRIT AND ALL UNDERSTAND-
ING AS SUPERMATTER COMES UNDONE
TO INTERPRET THE TRANSLATION AS:
"THE WORD DEVELOPED AS ITSELF ALONE"

7

ARTICLES OF SICKNESS BECOME COMMODIT-
IES INVESTING EACH LABOURER WITH UP-
BRINGING OR A SENSE OF LOSS: THAT LITTLE
SOMETHING THEY CAN'T QUITE PUT
INTO WORDS: HE'S GOT THE SEA IN HIS BLOOD
WILL MEAN EMBOLISM AND BRING DIS-
ASTER TO HIS FAMILY — TOO HONEST BY HALF
YOU'RE BLIND TO THE MACHINATIONS OF
THE MARKET, HANGING FROM A BLACK-
FRIAR'S WINDOW, IN SIGHT OF THE THAMES,
WHICH LIKE FLEET STREET IS PART OF THE
FLOW OF THE UNIVERSAL BODY WHOSE IN-
SOLVENT DEBTS CANNOT TRANSLATE INTO
THE BODY CORPORATE YOU'VE LIQUIDATED

8

THE SKILLED PRACTITIONER TURNS AS
WORDS BREAK ENCLOSURE AND SHINE
WITH A GRAVITATIONAL INTENSITY, TO
BURN AS THE STONE HUSHES THE VOICES
THOUGH THE CHOIR, IN SOLITUDE
ANALYSING THE SHAPE IN ITS COMPLETE-
NESS , THE VILE ARCHITRAVES MOULDING
AND THE THIN CURTAINS ORANGE WITH
TRAFFIC, THE FIRE UPSTAIRS A SHADOW OF
AN EVACUATION, THE PURGING OF
IMMEDIACY AND A STEPPING INTO THE
TREACHEROUS WETLANDS EXPLOSIVE WITH
BIRD LIFE [RARA AVIS] AS THE ROOM'S
ESSENCE SINKS WITH THE LOSS OF CRAFT

9

THE HOPE LIES IN THE READING AND NOT
ACCUMULATION OF WEALTH, THAT A PRE-
BABEL DOES NOT EXIST NAGS LIKE PILOT
FISH, AS IF CONTACT IS JUST BUILDING A
KEY TO UNRAVEL THE TEXT, BUT THIS IS DE-
VOID OF ASPIRATION OR FEAR JUST AS THE
WATERS BREAK AND THE RIVER DRIES UP —
IT'S LOST WITH BIRTH — THIS MOVING
TOWARDS A REMEDY AND THE ABSOLUTE-
NESS OF NUMBERS, INDEXED AGAINST THE
FACILITIES OF TONE, A BRILLIANT OBSER-
VATION; THE NIGHT HERON TRANSFORM-
ING AMONGST THE RICHES OF THE DARKEST
SWAMP, INFORMING ALL COSMOGONIES

10

DISTRIBUTION OF SURPLUS = TOLERANCE,
THE TOXICOLOGY CURING AS THE WEEDS
INVIGORATE, NO LONGER CLUTCH AT THE
HULL WITHOUT UNIAXIALLY PRECEDING
FIELDS UP STREAM AS IF SOUND INVEST-
MENT COMES AS REWARD FOR A PSYCHIC'S
TRANSFERENCE OF DERR-IDA'S LIFE INTO
YOUR OWN: *Mais notre poème ne tient pas en
place dans des noms, ni même dans des mots. Il
est d'abord jeté sur les routes et dans les champs,
chose au-delà des langues, même s'il lui arrive de
s'y rappeler lorsqu'il se rassemble, roulé en boule
auprès de soi, plus menacé que jamais dans sa
retraite: il croit alors se défendre, il se perd.*

Frame(d)
for Karl Wiebke

erosion mimics a frame
like the severed limb retained:
raison d'être a vacant twitch
of the lip, placed in such
& such a non-littoral, but
inner like litotes cut out
of bridgehead & speech & speculative
shoulds that lie beneath

water: praising all THAT
fraught like ambiguity,
yeh, just a series of cross-
hatching, tide & tessarae
gauges of temperature: flow-
set in solid shadows or float-
ed against the picaresque
as distance

otiose, no neat slabs
defining banks of algae
red as graffiti, the
ordinance of iron & water &
yes, over, over the bridge

interplay: they careen hulls
rotten of colour &
greedy for detail: light-
ships & deadbanked &
dead-eyed as they scrape non-
quant
itative modes of seeing, or shrouds
of dead eyes in the topsailed
balusters, we lean against the rail

where is it we see
this vast field of outers

        &

ravishing inners, smoothly
ravishing inners, smoothly
prized apart as text—UR
&

enjambent over & under
& only in disbelief
does the hardened bream
fisher accept his hollows
came with bridge & dredge
& steep vertical in-deep
but needing obviously to outdrift the damage
in defining or redefining or holding to task
the engineer did not think to glance beneath
            the gloss

we see from betwixt & hear AND, a visual mix like planes
as aerodones, refuse & list in curves the waves' trans-
lations as taken meanings, & we must taste the acrid frame,
but re-
            fuse to be drawn entirely

            THE as seals are scuppered, so so small
the tiny coda that eats the larger rotting fish:
            as embroidery to cerulean depth
& tableaux of scrutiny

Appendices

Syzygytics

1   Cosmic Conspiracy

Where thin-ended counter-
point makes good the poorly balanced
confrontations between the dead
& the living: abseiling reservoir fascias
& taking the pressure held
in the pub below locked-in Mun-daring
the smoke-filled valley they change
sheets daily & you pretend
you know (none)of them. Thunder-
heads close over as water & even dams
have tides like the suppression of meter.
This manipulation of scrutiny, factoring
the loose language as a rope snaps
or cleat frag-
men-tates like news
from nowhere.

2   Eureka!

Thank Fassbinder for Veronika Voss
& independence a kind of damage control: Atom
& Eve, "live in the elec-
TRICK
le gard-
ens of Eden" like a charm
of gold finches,
nomenclature is the pallid cuckoo
a semitone bird over the semi
corpses (the sea cranberry
with a touch of fairy wren

drinks only the flickering lustre
of historic plummage).
It's all narrative
really in White-
chapel

3   SUIT OF LIGHT

The matador's clothing
stunningly white (now)
as the body fluid
scuttles its own
fable: the subject de-
fines its truth as copy-rite.
Dead bulls in the North
ARE rational they tell you
in the North & belief
IS emphatic in the South.

4   ACROSTIC

conceit telescoped
as control is
subterranean or suggests
        carmon figuratum
though what we see
is op-
        (i)sition
[all]. small groupings of words
making ad-hoc com-
munication poss-ible.

5   STASIS & WANDER   (ING)

You cannot sustain
collecting sound
against your vigorous display
patrolling
your like-minded journeys
beyond us, as such,
suggesting variable
& versatile
time-tables. You're tide-
al.

6   STEPHEN FREDMAN: "THE DARK SIDE OF BROMIGE'S
ENTERPRISE IS ITS CANNIBALISM — A TRANSGRESSION WHOSE
IMPLICATION IS ALL ACTS OF CRITICISM OR TRANSLATION
BROMIGE BRINGS TO THE SURFACE."

in the new moon
the blood was thin
& the diaphragms
of cameras gaped
wide open hoping
to take the ALL in:
like Whitman
wandering
or letting lines
outrun the rhythm
& INCHOATE it IN
the plan for
freedom, as op-
possing libertine
as liberty,
re: Poe

& sickly,
not filled with aquatic
blood

plastic ripples & flaps
in the radiation,
wave on wave
like micro-coverings
in the nice new kitch-
en,
blown out & shed-down
the motion
strobing & apocalyptic
as sunlight
counters
this glut of words
with blocks
of words
that ARE small
-er, & exist
as trick or su-
ggestion> strips of plastic
repelling flies   oil on the hinges
shelling peas
floors slippery & language
meaning the word
in it[']s use

annotating
Canberra
Commonwealth Avenue
ACT 2600
tel 270 6666
interlocutor a meeting on the 2nd floor

[154]

of a flat white building, unable to get above
the smog
s
invidious sibbbbbbbbilllancccce > MAASTRICHT made in its
necessary imperialist fram
e
work
Logic bombing Ken Wong Computer Weekly
Managing Information Security. FUCK, who blew the cover?
:
["The Pandair Case in 1987 in-
    volved the (evolve)
in the case of alleged planting ("")

in a series of 3 (three) logic time bom
bs, contract (ed) systems programmers
on the freight company's steps
came down with a virus, in composition
i.e. London & Birmingham
[like vignettes of rose-light & focus
    cringing deeply in the heavy air:

Out of the stout air & sullen
masonry, I am drenched
in the thick rose-red light of God,
my veins hot with transfusion,
the cathedral the vibrant
heart, a bell massaging the dead
parts of the body with the sounds
of its light.

Or from the train the spindly minaret
or a thin mosque
holding its crescent
as a focus

on the cooling towers
of the power station: see no evil
hear no evil & speak no evil
reduced to nothing,
miniscule in the sweet
if shaky curve
that holds the steady eye
of God.]. the ef-
fects of the
          log-ic bomb
were to lock out
the syst-
em (ics) more than four terminals were in use or to
delete data
from a key area of the computer's working menu only & to cause
the system to crash on three separate (3) dates" complete
discursive articulation of dates as countering the points of sun
& moon & even at night the river is golden & exsubceit as
Silliman whens language as moving capitalist tangibly in the in
& referentiality
as narrowed
in the
funct-
ION,
retro
cracking the strained vocal chords so language is simply
breath painted as movement on-
to the face
like the floor of the ocean spliced with the highest point
conceivable
of or in the
sky: Freud might say we wake yawning & zipping & spent
& that is so. offset the lens
as telescope.
we see the stars zipping about.

WE don't want your warships here & diffidently proclaim
fall-rise & rise
as ~~sunning~~ on the beach you real-
ize
it(s) night
& yell only to yourself, for god(s) sake(s) get up
imperatively structural & <u>stressing</u> the guy with
a metal detector <u>will</u> have a ball with your steely corpse
in the early morning moonlight, as Fowler grossly
if fluent-
ly might put it:
- = Bold   a sentence has a surface structure
        formed by transformations of a
    semantic deep structure consisting of a
modality component plus a propositional component
                the latter based on a
    predicate attended by one or more nouns
            in different roles

~~exordium~~

auxiliaries

        give us Gorgias star studded in his tunic
flamboyant stylist
rhetoretician
or Protagoras teaching as taught the lie as TIME
morphemically
& quibbling
phonotactically pitched phonemed 1234

"spring tide, tide of maximal range, near the time of new and full Moon when the Sun and Moon are in syzygy—i.e., aligned with the Earth. Conjunction is the time during new Moon when the Sun and Moon lie on the same side of the Earth; opposition is the syzygy condition that occurs during full Moon when the Sun and Moon are positioned on opposite sides of the Earth. In either case of syzygy, the tide producing forces of the Sun and Moon reinforce each other, and the tidal amplitudes on Earth are at their greatest . . . "

(i)   TAROT

(ii)   OPPOSITION

in the wreck of love you bloom
though cannot write this,
both are here, ménage à trois,
tryst tryst the river sings its
gravely deepened tidal swing

(iii)   WORD

"illustrious zodiac"
where are you now?
water's out
& no reflection
to follow

(IV)   CONJUNCTION

() () () : hear that?
the sun speechless
& the moon sibilant
& the earth   tremulously
solid.

9 STOCK EPITHET

Calvert Watkins: "As early as 1854, the great German Classical
Philologist Theodor Bergk recognized that the Homeric
poems represented not the beginning of Greek poetry, but
indeed the zenith, the complete fulfilment of the possibili-
ties of epic verse."

inertia & amplitude in the tremulous surge
inertia & amplitude in the tremulous surge

inertia & amplitude

in the
trem- u -lous   surge

10 CATCALL OR AP-
PLAUSE?

1 > 4

bi-nomial

hedge & bet lounge circular
as deflect, a night in front
of the television a night
fully balmed & glowing

the silver screen of cyclone mesh

(the brain-eaters emerge from the cone's
perfect (ly)   linear time frame)
no comparison in or with a gloriously
un - spectacular flight as ibis lifts from rose   byte
bushes
& old arguments mulch & lull

timbre

                              paste photo here

the fall in ratings but yu
claw yr way back!
                4   1
laissez faire a perennial apparition of the backwaters

some coot on the deck getting his hands wet

                        fading with the shadows
of boats

masthead, flag, emblem

[160]

11 12 SCALE, A-TONAL, CALYPSO

twenty eights, rosellas, regents, smokies, red-cappeds, grass,
& blue-bonneted parrots, lark and magpie, foxes and cats, all
link up: slow mice   as the owl burst

the moon like the sun in their tiny
eyes
all dead on the York to Williams road,
all dead on the York to Williams road,

inner-lights without a coast
slow stretched in the dimming
mostly broke as spark in fox-dry bristle
as corrugations a-ramble & you are there too
but not behind the wheel: roughing
the jackknifed   the broken-headed tracks
fishtails dead as flattened
batteries,
constellations of ghost gums
smugging their torn van-
ity

12 CYBERNETICS

here feedback king
fishes & waits to be   poise as pause
a hesitation
undoing the chain which could nev-
er be
role

            per
                role

in the system be
fed & fed & fed
back [King] the king
is reg, on-side,
the death of very small
fish

13 STEERAGE

in the method
it was hellishly wet
& they didn't know
where they were head-
ing, burnt as heat-seeking
or maybe lazar printing
the vicious swell: uncertainty certainly controlled so well
from up there on the bloody bridge, up & adam, rebuild
& get a neo-country moving with a different motion,
the sea unusually calm, rough in the steerage

14 CUSP, THE DERRIDA OF GRAMMATOLOGY

he <u>him</u> to himself who logocentristically
moves like "the one who will shine" is STILLED
as he between the two she(s) of his
possessiveness, summing the written-up
metaphysics, which IS that
easy
as Rousseau gloriously says via derri-
da la la la "une importance
a laquelle elle n'a pas
droit" as revoking Brodsky's
"anthologies of American poetry should be sitting there ... next to

the Bible." and who knows the he he he in love.

or:

para-sailing & dumped
on the chop like lines
cut low in saturated
froth shred-decked & tail-
kited like flapping cloth
& this has been written differently elsewhere by the same auth-
or without a(ny) different meaning. like the arcs sky-stoned

& welded from heaven, this a planetarium,
where the resonant moon de-
centralizes

the modifying of
cognitive structures

REPETITION

repetition does not make poetry but
repetition is memory to make sense of the inputs which is
way poetry is actually against repetition and any-thing
vaguely mnemonic & those poets who set out with purpose
& are consumed by form & function or are victims of page
sizes & notions of line length trying to justify their presence
at the next canonization can't be writing poetry
for they are in fact making sense despite their slavery to
treacherous metaphor which hides all data in its non-
specifics like a fog or a poison-
ous fish lurking near the shore of

rhetoric

substituting events which are absent

on the wading beach as if sent out by
some central all-powerful notion distorted only by our inability to read
through the density of water
though a poem or poisoning shaped
as P-O-E-T-R-Y would bring proof
to the claim through announcement or advertising like frozen confect-
ions on a hot salty beachhead or the
stimulus that comes out through yelling repeatedly at blood tastes re
vealing (later) the poison of the stonefish but does this make it po-
try? in the continual recall of every
thing that might well be a flow amongst the currents of thought already in
as much as we can have a language outside the empirically driven it
matters not a damn that

stimulus

retrieval: moving towards Gestalt

that the stonefish stung you or rather that you unable to see
through water as the sun was at a slight angle of midday . . .
though collective knowledge helps in that identification
makes treatment more likely to succeed so the poem cannot
be written unless the chemicals assisting recovery make
sounds on contacting the poison, the administering of the
poison might also be sound-driven & distinctly rhythmic
though the body shut-down by pain probably has little knowl-
edge of it—the repetition of the original scream is muffled by
narcotics & that shock to the vocal chords hangs as the poem

all information has been previously stored & song
is exclusive of nature

    spontaneous & uninterrupted by thought & the pain
diminishing reminds you of pain & its implications & the impli-
cations of stonefish & beaches & adverts & water & how keep-
ing out of the sea denies language its autonomy

The Radnoti Poems

Eclogue On An Aerial Photograph

That asked you'd say
it was just in a day's labour,
the fields rolling out
of synch, like clocks
on a watertower, the photograph
the disembodied sight
lapsed into the past.
That's what it's like,
your place from up here—
windmills collusive
on the earthen walls of dams,
crops brassy in sunlight,
fielding idylls as the plane
crops the flight plan.

Field Glasses

"there is no device to reveal such things with accuracy"

It's because this happens
in absence, the larger movements
as obvious as tractor marks
in the muddy paddocks,
or the wind furrowing channels
in dry country: a kind of
microcosm embellished, the invisibles
glowing like monozite, the distance
nothing

population surges, terracing
the hills, even ironing them out
filling swamps reclaiming land
from the sea hidden in the
observation from <u>here</u>, as the tableau
looks as clear as it might be,
and the equipment of our
occupation moves forward

flight optics as surveillance
or launched as Landsat 1 or 2
multispectral images,
the composite colour bands
concentrating indifference
in the likely, as hydrographers
divine the seasonal adjustments,
flowing with the expected bonuses,
as clear as insider trading,
de-briefing the close-ups

Edmund Burke
as if to focus on an errant
partner's features without
their knowing will reveal
a truth suspected or desired,
the *I is an other*
the *I is* another
I am enlarging in the self
of reflexivity, threatening
self preservation
sublimely

Fontainebleau
so deeply etched as stark an ochre
image as the dialect could command
in bringing clarity to its composition:
that lacklustre empirical harmonizing,
analogy sans transcript persistent
in the gleaned enlightened rationale:
poetry is persistence

the desirability of seeing
before arrival, plagiarizing
the future and brochuring
as distance, libellous misgivings
as naked they strut the beaches
these our antipodean [noble]
savages

as sight degenerates
and the light objectifies
the crested grebe
moves out of range

Bluff Knoll Sublimity

for Tracy

1.

The dash to the peak anaesthetizes
you to the danger of slipping as the clouds
in their myriad guises wallow about
the summit. The rocks & ground-cover
footnotes to the sublime. The moods
of the mountain are not human
though pathetic fallacy is the surest
climber, always willing
to conquer the snake-breath
of the wind cutting over
the polished rockface,
needling its way through taut
vocal cords of scrub.

2.

It's the who you've left behind
that becomes the concern as distance
is vertical and therefore less inclined
to impress itself as separation; it's as if you're
just hovering in the patriarchy
of a mountain, surveying
the tourists—specks on the path
below. Weather shifts are part of this
and the cut of sun at lower altitudes
is as forgiving as the stripped
plains, refreshingly green at this time
of year. You have to climb it because it's
the highest peak in this flat state,
and the "you have to" is all you

can take with you as statement
against comfort and complacency:
it's the vulnerability that counts up here.

3.

You realize that going there to write a poem
is not going there at all, that it's simply
a matter of embellishment, adding
decorations like altitude,
validating a so so idea
with the nitty gritty of conquest.
Within the mountain another
body evolves—an alternate
centre of gravity holding
you close to its face.
From the peak you discover
that power is a thick, disorientating
cloud impaled by obsession, that
on seeing Mont Blanc—THE POEM—
and not Mont Blanc—THE MOUNTAIN—
the surrounding plains
with their finely etched topography
can be brought into focus.

Aspects Of The Pagan

"there/blossoms precious flesh and after"

we call it a Thursday, harvesting lust
in the public of trees, investigating
the drop into the black hole of verdure
in Italy and Upper Palatinate: Nider, Friuli,
Kemnnat: Ember day souls in purgatory
on display, the Carlo Ginzberg(ian)
furious horde, women leading with
generous thighs, journeying motif
under the direction of Abundia-Satia-
Diana-Perchta, impervious to pricks
the Ember Days of Christmas, those hordes
of early deaths or those as precise
as the mathematics of crop circles
in the glades of Norman Lindsay

in the glades of Norman Lindsay
the red shift shows receding galaxies
of attendant sycophants, the halls
of Australian poetry, only annular
eclipses possible in this short of breath
salutation, the dark eyed copse sullen
in snow glowing as inversion the fields
of summer grain and exaltation as the last
circle is cut and fed into the waiting hopper
into the tardis belly of the little grassbird
and in turn the belly of a goshawk or near
the sullen wetlands that of the swamp harrier,
that just below the exuberant trappings
surfaces echo like coronas, the yawn of lust

surfaces echo like coronas, the yawn of lust
a dark herald on the heaths and commons
of enjambment | considered as backdrop
to the *goings-on* and dragging of chains
and obelisks through particularly verdant
chunks of scrubland, the Georgic bounty
of a new arcadia laboured in the glossies
and saturating television: as if in looking up
they'd be blinded, transfixed and burnt
to the tender core, as embellishment
or reduction in the wickedary as returning
the small sweet wonders have us lapping
at the vanishing fragrance, the pressings
of a drunken strain, an allergy to pollen

of a drunken strain, an allergy to pollen
they wedded gaily around the sundial:
a skull-capped wedding in the overflowing
gardens, a skull-capped garden as the oldest
ritual, and despite the searing post-ecliptic
sun drawing driven sap greenly against
the hessian backdrop, you wander by
and are welcomed, the plosive voice of festive
luring, as if the skin of decorum were
stripped—écorché—the beautiful flesh
vigorously working against the designs
of history, that language works against
a repetition, though seems lacking
in the dying breath, the riot of roses

in the dying breath, the riot of roses
clans against a precocious talent} a-drift
the seamy escapades of romantic jest,
the forlorn mutability of lush nights
on the rockface, high in the imperative
alps, or south, among the peaks
of the Stirling Ranges, where voices
confuse location and the heady fall
to forgotten places: a murmur
of this mysterious and awful doubt
in the glades of Norman Lindsay:
surfaces echo like coronas, the yawn of lust,
of a drunken strain, an allergy to pollen
in the dying breath, the riot of roses

Akbar

"I'm truly sorry man's dominion
Has broken Nature's social union . . . "
ROBERT BURNS

The swarming things swarm in the wall space as heavy
as liquid concrete the flawed wall fast collapses,
spilling out all is unclean in the bright sunlight
as they dash crazily into dusk, carcass on
seed so sown but wet seed and carcass as unclean
as geckoes hesitate over Leviticus
and then Samuel, guilt offering of five golden
tumours and five golden mice as the ark comes back
to solve the ills of plague, cantankerous sheep with
their stomachs bloated, the salt scars and the torn creeks,
the dozer on its rippled tracks cutting a new
road through the last stand of trees and the mice bursting
up out of paddocks and into silos and through
hessian and polyurethane sacks and into
houses—testing cupboards and children's beds, the cats
sick of the flesh of mice so satiated they
run scared from the seething blankets, the kids filling
holes with buckets of water and blasting ratshot,
crazy with buckets and lengths of polythene pipe,
every sheet of corrugated iron bubbling
like molten zinc, galvanised under the harsh white
moonlight, a collusion of seasons, the climate
just right, the parthenogenesis of brash top soil,
the tunnels the vessels carrying rich sustenance
to a shrivelling surface. As now ideas too
full for allotted space spill into the nervous
system like mercury, thought the stimulant to
a flurry of possibilities, a smiting
plague that eats away at the store of plump seed grain
collected from the fullest heads in the densest
crops on ground rich with nurturing—that no planning

or safeguards could prevent such a dark collusion
of seasons, of heat, of moisture, of a bumper
year it's avowed . . . but that's after the trap's been sprung!
So now the mice moving in their millions devour
with one mind, consuming the body of the earth,
squeezing through its pores, filling even space between
particles, until they become the one body,
the akbar of myth, the unclean creature that is
the flesh, the breath; that is the progeny of dirt.

Stone Midden

Extract of transported heritage
the deep-earth tap of old world
fertility, heaped high over the cash
crop, the lush astro-turf of the
twentieth century, soil living
on borrowed time, feigning health
like a recently sanctified ritual.
This cone of refuse stacked around
a broken finger of rock, mockingly
chthonic, landmark on a family
property, a greying negative
atrophied in recent memory.
That we don't know what land
it regulates, it suggests
familiarity. From somewhere
in the area. That despite its deep
age that it might appear
in any paddock, glowering
over the florescent fall-away,
or in high summer, emphasizing
the indifference of the exposed
topsoil. This last rubbishy
petrification of old land,
of thick scrub, of a lookout
to survey the fruits
of fire-stick farming.

Of Writing At Wheatlands

1.

Asked about the wandoo
and what it signifies: the spirit,
hollowing trees struck and cast
as didgeridoos, the ghosts
of a burnt yellow landscape
gloating over aneurisms
in the waspish air,
and the redgum, blood of the earth,
clustering thickly on the lower ground,
staining Arcadia with its brutish sap.
And the magpie lark reversing
into the path of a charging car
as stooks render patronizing
the effete comments of continuance,
as the oppressed, the insignificant,
glow rewardingly in successful
forecast, a longing increased
with the familiar patterns
of recall: the death of the crop,
the harvest, the errant blue wren
defying geographies, as if an idyll
is possible, while downwind a trail
of devastated pink and grey galahs
destroys the imagery, the sky's
many bands of film,
each with its different
and untruthful qualities,
the drill bit biting deep
into chalky dirt, dry
is *recherché*, is the notional exile
you impose upon yourself
as if you have a choice.

[187]

2.

a small bird's frightened feather
informs the screen and lustrous
is the kodachrome of labour,
the sweat on the bare backs
of the worker, the occasional
smile out of context, and home
they go well satisfied they've
seen it as it is, the bird
somewhere else: plummeting

3. THE TRANSLATIONS ARE ABSORBED: ORGANICALLY

stones skipping across the dam
in the tonal languages
of investment, it's what
you can't give up

of not rendering something that has intrinsic beauty
into something that would acquire beauty

would you stop denying
and in those moments
reach for a similar idyllicism?

It's as if you want to anoint
this place again,
as if you had this place
despite its fences

: to lay the gridwork
over the particulars as value
<u>should</u> be added with imperial
measurement

like duration,
the clot of sand re-welded
in every incantation,
the frozen framework
of title deeds in a place
so hot the salt looks cold enough
to weld touch to its glittering surface,

though seasonal change
retains always the essence of the

as we en-DUR{ATION}
measure against our spatial
configuration

5. A Letter Written In Earlier Life To Your Future Wife

Prep land for seeding
in late night fox ochre
and Deleuze in the spotlight
having none of its flamboyance
in the moment of concentrated
undertaking, the collaboration
of disk and moisture
after the first rains,
and the dragging of an exploiting
culture across the bones
and viscous remains of:
the red bark the fox of the one wheel in line
introducing the thud of pistons and sounds
in clay churned as clods,
the *boondies* of childhood
like stolen nouns
beneath the local transfer
that beyond the cramped conditions
in the tractor's cabin
there is always conveyance
of another nature:
a darkly changing aspect

Calendar: a <u>continuous</u> narrative

"Just look around . . . you'll see wonders"

JUNE

Our year starts here, a dank
wet South, dust dry
North. In between, there's
nothing definitive. But being
an inflection of *your* climate
we'll remain as far under
as possible.

JULY

The trees here that are bare
are European with few exceptions.
The widow maker sits glumly
though retains its foliage.
In summer it absorbs moisture
and drops limbs [<u>indifferently</u>]
now only cold winds cut
its mordant flesh.

AUGUST

diagnostically the limitations
of winter strain the capacity
of the power grid, storms
lacerate the Unions
and Jim is hot-under-the-collar
outside Parliament.

SEPTEMBER

The boat people
are still incarcerated
in the Port Hedland
Detention Centre,
Land Rights Claims
are choking the courts
into inactivity,
the mining companies
are doing deals
on the side,
the oil brews
in the Timor Gap.
Amongst the peonies
and daisies blue leschenaultia
is blooming.

OCTOBER

Carpets of everlastings
are lifted from the scrub
and relaid in city mansions.

NOVEMBER

They're harvesting in some places now,
at least in the central wheatbelt,
deeper south the crops are still green
and it will be Christmas to the New Year
they're working. The calendar
being particular to location,
like the markings on seed packets,
the stimulants to growth.

DECEMBER

Cyclone Frank is off the West Coast
and cyclone Emma is hitting Christmas Island.
That's North, but the fallout reaches you here
eventually. Sullen weather,
that threatens to jam
two climatic zones
together. On either side
of the degenerative low
it's stinking hot.

JANUARY

Month of the Republic.
The beaches full
and lashings of zinc cream
staining the sea.
The sun so harsh you dare not expose
your skin on clear days between
ten and three, or if you're into denial,
saying *it can't happen to me*,
between eleven and two.
A national bronzing,
a cargo cult in melanomas.

FEBRUARY

Sometimes on a sultry evening
the harsh dry compresses
into a sudden rush of perspiration,
thunderheads

build over the river and break
with a flurry of lightning,
the shattered luminescence
of obscured, swallowed sun.

Cameras on the foreshores attempt
to capture the definitive etching,
pyrographic over the purple
skies like indelible pencil.

The wetlands scorched and irritable,
deep below the watertable wallows,
the bush firebrigades on the city's outskirts
on high alert, sinking heaps of beer.

MARCH

Congestion stalks the initial
windfalls like haiku full blown
with humidity but then with a sudden
rush of heat struck dumb, desiccated,
wizened under the insistent sun.

APRIL

A sultry month, but the nights
are often chill. There is little balance
between outside and inside atmospheres.

MAY

A May election is not technically possible
but the mood if it were would be unforgiving,
driven against the zones of comfort
in the hardenings of the coming winter.
A referendum's like capital punishment
but it's pretty mild here comparatively,
they call it *Mediterranean*,
in this Yued place, matrilineal moieties,
patrilineal descents grouped locally, Nyungars
incarcerated for stealing the not so golden fleece.

The Rust Eclogues: Radnoti, Poetry, and
The Strains of Appropriation

(I) AUTOECIOUS

the appropriation of a host
in the random dispersal
of words, hard investments
in the soft tissue
of national identity,
the singular mind is the passion
of heritage, the aspect of blood,
the notion hosting
the struggle, the call up
of the one body on which the soul
is parasite enough, as if there's
a need to talk with the words
you live off, their buzzing growth,
their singular obsession
with death as seasonally
significant
in this and more, as if you
couldn't say this is THE
auto da fé, as if accrued
love would be filed, "I" with this single
species shall examine need,
and as the host grows wizened
the spores make as if airborne
delivering yesterday's news
you are only living
through the communications
with a self that offloads
a myriad of voices
into autopilot, collecting
black box data
obsessively,

that internally
the dark cell
can't disappoint,
like dialogue
between soul and self
and the conceits
of biotechnology,
as if safe from an informing
segmented space,
as if no one looks in
on solitary, as all
surveyed remonstrate
with the instant view
of the multitudes: spores
anatomical, political,
well disciplined.

(II) HETEROECIOUS

Riven in the folds and clefts
like envy
it increasingly absorbs light
and wallows on moist days
harbouring tetanus
and rendering food crops
and collections of Hungarian
postage stamps
worthless, all hosts mutable
and fair game; its refrain
is soundless
and yet it reverberates
through all industry,
keeping the bastards honest
or sending them broke,

incorporating the oxidation
of nutrition and wealth, the symbols
of growth edging out the lustrous crop
as a fantastic collusion
of season and labour,
the lyrical eyes standing
linear and outside,
itself, no longer reliable
in the newly-made contexts,
become the compound adjective
in its manipulation
from past participle, like the gender
indiscretions of bread-making
from the very same nineteenth
century strain of wheat, maybe
from the fields of metaphor,
or cross-fertilized
in the language laboratory,
the leering investigative eyes
of the ag. department.
Sharecropping
as dross around the mouthpiece,
the seamy vigilante-ism of the press,
the glittering surfaces
defecting like layers
on layers of hate,
just being lesser degrees
of love in the conscription
of appropriate doctrines
to good feeling, the indulgences
they call appropriation,
the well feds of American
poetry, the wells where sound is absorbed
and yet rings in the water appear;
the reddish brown surface

discolouration
is the racism of words
as the weather hums
a few bars of a heritage
listing. Jealousy driving
the creative urge, poetry
the spiritualism of the material
religions. A few chips or flakes
in a test-tube, a glassine
envelope, the chart
in the sampler's hut,
the glamorous intrusions
of popular culture on old-ish
negatives, the consternations
of hyperspace outing random
associations of alliterative infestations,
the escape velocity, the mass of a star,
against poetry, which is like
an Elizabethan village showing
the old arts, no longer
cells watched over by
the commercially fetishized,
the contracted panopticon
is the lookout, and all is one,
and the profits roll if in the greater
stack the rust is diluted
and sold off before it can take hold,
consolidate, thicken, colonize,
procure, absorb, digest,
consume, render even the highest
quality product worthless. Ro-
tating the expansion
we contract the better half
like sharecropping,
documenting the common

[200]

identity, the self
of nationhood though some
of the we having cleaner hands
and bribing the sampler.
The stack is cleared
or dispersed beyond
the edges of the map, and that's that.
A new season, a stainless steel
multi-voiced and glamorous
factory. A spectacle!

Empire and Roundhouse

"Just yesterday the sky and the sea
were welded on the distant horizon
in a long kiss . . . "

After months at sea narrowing
to the dodecagram
like metrics, the patterning
of sentences forecasting
words scribbled
in-thumbprint, graphing
the i.d. of satellites balancing guilt
architecturally
with landlocked vestiges of empire
all in stone

of: looking out to prisoners
who are stacked
against the sea, lines
charting the equanimity
of guards as the territories
of Bohemia and Hungary
are added to the Habsburgs' already considerable
territories, but this colony
of convicts is a consequence

of the sea, the tradewinds
and currents, so even here
they can only hear and smell
spray, locked
in-the-round, blank walls locked
in global
consolidation as local tribes
are ground idyllically
and nobly into the visual plane, the
stone art

of warden, governor
and whale blubber
dragged through the tunnel
of commerce
and viability and profit,
of langue and parole
down here, as reminisce, up there
the impossible
glint of a malicious sun displaced
from Pirano

on the Adriatic or even the White
Cliffs of Dover
during a heatwave, here a harsh
blue roof
as nearby the river meanders
silently,
like a vacation in midday's
white glare,
the twilit cells yesterday, just
yesterday

The Colony of Libertatia
southbound
from Madagascar, virtuously
assigned
like a pitted cenotaph
and stone brig,
a moral state in which Gregor
Mendel's
experiments facilitate [though]
historically

the sweet pea flower grows rank
in flower
boxes of port officials,
not a crack in the limestone
allowing even
for a stray
seed to lodge and grow,
recombining genes
on the evented chromosomes
as traits

of criminal class(es)
are concentrated
into
notoriety [the:] like Mayakovsky
making verses
with forms, or bricks,
architectonically
sailing out of the quay
with the dreamy irony
of the retiring bourgeoisie, a home-

made
concrete boat that defies
the bottom,
the theme too big and too complex
as he sizes [them] up, building,
distributing ambiguities
concisely, though it's hard too
to maintain a sense of humour
when you're chained
sixteen in a twelve by six cell, only

the uncinus
clouds hooking their way
into the doorframe,
degrading speech with their
goading clauses,
so much so that darkness
has them saying
there is no night, there's
an absence of daylight,
but there is no night

"but there <u>do</u> live ... "}
here too, here they live impervious
to history: as tonals:
special and absolute and relative
and retrograde
in collapsing simultaneity,
the loveless tryst
of heritage distributed
"out of rumours and worms"
in a kissless sleep

as institutional: here in peace
Georget and Chaumie and Foucault
only as metonym in and of N.
Harou-Romain, a-hoy
The Maison centrale at Rennes
and Stateville USA, enclaves
of freedom in Whitechapel, Ann
Arbor, Serbia and Budapest,
sighting clans of totemic landfall
on the dark white bow spit of Fremantle.

A Zone Essay On Prohibition and Purity

Scrutiny discouraged or forbidden, the polluted privilege
flowing dissolute across: hard water that sticks and breaks
down only silent dirt, the anxious metaphors, access
as privilege in the landsat designated open spaces,
closed in small but concentrated openings, as poets
labour in innocence in wrath, trans the substance
of drink and counter meals in pubs on the main highway,
up the banner to catch the eye of the tv camera,
we drink our fences though some buy filters or drums
of mineral water at service stations, despite our privilege
reason qualifies stability as deeper deeper into the dope-infested
dark dank forest they go, towards the ochre banks
and flat blue tableaux, zoning in emergent chemicals
like rancid paraphernalia in the political act: take
the prophetic gravel landscape as only rangers do
as monks in Meteora or at Qu'mran or the caves
of Saint Anthony testing theories of abjection & temptation
without resonance, not a sound to be had spreading
colloquially out in the rising flood of scape, of tableau,
of dehydration in the place where water cannot be drunk
for purity's sake. Here the I redefines its place
and splits itself as process, the rapid oxidation, the gas
as haze just above the delinquent surfaces, the signed
public spaces, focussing as nationhood the mutual place
like boastful decadence, hysterical in the priming
of labels against Gabriele d'Annunzio plagiarizing
the sacred texts, against the artistry of a degenerate
world lying in wait, redgum sap levered from the massive
trunk with a long knife in South Dandalup, nearby
the narrowing spillway and blue mechanics of the flood-
gates, control-column fluted and space-aged
and off limits, ruminating over the window of the dam,
"the fascist glorification of the inhuman" quoting
against the likely source, as the streams still slip
from seams in rock, the under-divined runnels

beneath the deforming forest floor, spores of bracken fern
falling like quotes in the need for pure appropriations,
the common body of water placing itself at zero
in the tremor filled anti-resilience of blasted air,
birds erupting East as the front moves nearer
and refugees move into prohibited zones: as one MAN
hits the blaster [principium individuationis] against
Hazchem and 1080 foxbait and the repetition of signs
Warning Conveyor   Bauxite Mining   Blast Area
                    PROHIBITED ZONE
as understated rust-red foliage placates the crowns
of republican trees in a dying forest. Purity as intent.
They drink clean water. Company planes and pilots
tracking souls on long-lease tracks, per tonne
the complete freedom of association in the company
newsletter. Mythos as letterhead the signs warning
you not to enter. Rebellion as bluster in the lonely
drought, those dry nights without constellations.
Who owns what in whose memory: "Now death
is blowing through the trees" reconstituted by rain.

Poems Without ~~Without~~ Radnoti

for Tracy and Juno

> *"O dear friend, how I've shivered with cold from the thought of this poem,*
> *standing in fear of the word, so that even today I have fled it.*
> *Half-lines were all that I wrote."*

1. AS IF THE SKY COMPOUNDS THE SHIFT

It's quite private this stretch
of the glare sharpened river

as if the sky compounds
the shift in your forced

into being there while
I'm here & comfortable, here

by choice, happy with
what I'm not. The lyrical eye

is blind with this light,
and it's the lingering

darkness behind the veneer
that suggests forcing

the image from nightmare
to nightmare, as steep as climbs

into weathered emptiness—
the forested hills across a water

protected against all incursions,
for the light is allowed to enter

this, the darkest of rooms,
is here by choice.

2. INTRUSIONS

It's like you can displace
the impending as the breeze

stiffens & the old world pylons
are silhouettes of their newer selves—

sinking deeper into the mud,
this talk of intrusion & the I

as another, as if you see
from inside the poem as it

should turn about an audience
of swamp harriers following

the boats back to the jetties,
the hill's corona like an articulation

of what romanticism might have been
in its European wrappings,

the mountains still invested
with their Arcadian trappings,

the evening inked hard against
the polished stone, the sculptured gardens.

3. The bird rapacious

(1)

That the moving cameras
might come and reel in doc-

umentary style the dawn, following
the river postman as coldly

as a cognitive template
allows the map it stoically insists;

but what am *I* doing
in the story, in Sophie Calle's

Suite vénitienne & Jean Baudrillard's
Please follow me, the city

in the wild place's tenure & tenancy,
the compelled ritual and power,

the superlatives of a recorded history
& "the secret of this enigmatic solicitation"

& revisionism in the silty depths,
hydraulics in our observations

squeezing the liquid essence
of vista, like quantum mechanics

paralleling our snap decisions
beneath the great and warmish Southern Skies:

an order of multiple fadings
in and out of a faceted picture.

(II)

The gurgle of the bird rapacious
amongst the rigour of trees

foiled against catastrophe regrowth
still struggling from the greatest

of bushfires, this the letter to my wife
made here, far south from a room in Cambridge

where sketchbooks of jealous interpretations
suggested, mise-en-scène, the traffic

amidst the conjured buildings,
the solidity of the coldest stone,

to be lost now in this antipodean space,
I witness to their demise

as all but idea or conceit against
the rapacious bird I can't describe.

4. THE SENSE OF BONDING IN THE NOTIONAL FLOW

The imperishable in Deleuze
is not the relative attitude

of his unavailability
for *tête à tête* or interview,

in the West <u>as place</u> & not idea
we don't endure what we never hear,

we measure in duration our initiation
to remain uninformed, while against

ourselves we lack comparison:
in essence we ARE open to change

though in tendency
stick together.

When Radnoti wrote; "It's Fall.
They're beating hazel nuts down

in the stalls/ the stillness seeps from the walls./
The dreamy pigeon perched by your neck, let it fly;/

the forest edges closer, the autumn leaf
falls/ the edge where the field meets

the sky/ falls too; you can hear the soft sigh."
he was bonded to the flux of notion.

It's Spring. The swollen air
brings on your asthma.

5. THE FOAMING CUT OF THE RUN-ABOUT

The verandah frame does not contain
the dazzling prospect of imagery—the actualities

dipped in scenes like grasping molecules:
the constant addition to rings of hydrogen

and carbon. The fossil-fuel effluent
that marbles above solution,

dispersed only by the foamy cut
of the run-about.

6. About the tides

What did you Radnoti know about the tides?
Did you glimpse in the image the loss of depth,

the enjambment of the articles, the displacement
of surfaces elongated with gravity.

Did pre-war fields of yellowing grain
lean towards the years of famine & depravity,

hunger like a mullet stranded in primal mangroves
on these occupied & fatal shores.

As the river moves out in glimpses
it's supplanted by the increments of depth,

oyster racks laid bare like the eviscerated
anatomies of more intricate creatures.

Sontag's democratizing of beauty
foams like witness to your "And that's

how you'll end too", the white-
wash of freedom thrilling

like a mix of mud and blood,
the white flesh of oysters

drying coldly just below
the hesitant waterline.

Radnoti Quarantine: Razglednicas

The way those poems were more than familiar
with death, soaking fluid from the corpse, absorbing
the mud. Those postcards from the last suffocated
breath, as if composed *deep* in the ground, recalling
tableaux and movements of people on a closing
landscape, where just below the dark surface you lay,
feeling their last hesitant movements, *their* forced march.
Those mountains bringing God no closer—elements
of the sublime drowned in their own words, that you might
have said look now to the journey of the tiny
shepherdess as she moves with the ripples of cloud
over the small lake's surface, but send no postcards . . .
For I have read those you carefully wrote before
your last march, receiving them an age after they
were sent, long after you had set off—history
franking them with blood and mud. Now they have burrowed
into the rot of a collective conscience filled
with readings of war—that footage from Vietnam
where the officer shoots the VC in Saigon
straight through the head, the cameras rolling as blood
rolled onto the street and spread like a small dark lake
that would not be stilled . . . Fifty years later the same
traffic stumbles through the Balkans, and CNN
is there moving where it can while others quietly
tell themselves to *just lie still.* Purnell's *History
of The Second World War* [I] explored as a child,
with images of humans and pack animals
caught exposed on thrombotic arterial roads
that had finally burst, churned into the soil's rank
garden . . . When that road reared and whinnied like a horse
taut as guns thundered from out of Bulgaria . . .
Hesitating, I glance up towards an outcrop,
a heron splendidly awkward in its roosting
tree, hunched and primal over the dark swamp water:
poets aren't silent now, but the guns are behind

newspaper print, lurking in layer on layer
of tv and computer monitor screens, deaf
to their own presence like flocks of terrible birds
smothering the persistent voice of the heron
as it rises again and again, long after.

The Benefaction

Vicissitudes on Interior

Prologue

They claim to preserve
the species from extinction

per vanitas in the prologue
or boundary stones

iron age in the central vein,
as reaching out they came

& circumnavigated the frame,
the inland sea deep within;

as the globe evolves
in articulation of its gardens,

hemispheric combination
of observation and inquiry,

charting prosperity,
Providence in rest position,

the needle idling
on its magnetic bed,

epiphanic utterance
as authenticity

decays despite the specific
population, emphatic industry,

the tightened line beneath
the constant rays of sun;

specimens and souvenirs,
governments of manuscripts

compiled pseudo and fragmentary,
the bone pits "La Cueva de los Guanches ... "

as if the song were your own
and the land were your refuge.

Brilliant, this mock sun
of the eastern horizon

to disappear and yet reappear
less visible, while West

the sun follows
        its double image,

children of a sullen country
sacrificed below.

            Slaves speak
intoning pagan Portuguese

and the stars brightening,
the luxuriant foliage expanding

magnificently,
        with variety

and trade burgeoning
in Bahai. A plague of flies

luminous over the uniform
procession of waves,

the slave futures in specimens
as collation and hypothesis

as the storm wracks the rigging,
the albatross's circumspection.

Lyner—rhizomic schooner—
bloated with 31 sheep 19 goats 6 dogs

sails munificently on
as water snakes

work the tools
                    and instruments.

Passage One

THE SANDSTONE RIM, LUXURIANT

1.

Through shoals of sand and shell
an island quarter turns

its anxious eye, tightly bound
red rock and green mud,

as on: the cliffs and broken beaches,
thinly-capped ridges of sandstone

as prospective marginalia, as suggested.
The confusion of loose disorder

augments the sand painting,
resuscitates

the fractious air: those trills
of evocation that resist

this prosody, this fringe
of grizzled vegetation:

the dogs dying from de-
hydration.

        The vernacular
isotropic: ring of stones,

central fire, as specific
and historical as line breaks,

as Corporal Cole's or Lushington's
enthusiasm for water,

the men crazy with despair,
the beehive architecture

of a reflexive language of protest
reverberating against the musket's

recoil, as the tide tears
with obvious irony, the codes

outside our echoing
idiolect, beyond

the nomadic discourse.
Mr Grey, Mr Grey . . . drink.

Sunrise slices the gorge
open to the basin,

as the conversation
of parakeet and cinnamon hawk

soothes the green ants' sting,
the opening forest

of pandanus and wild nutmeg
emphasising the absence

of media speculation,
the otherness.

A storm came with night
& the schooner seethed off the coast.

In the name of Her Majesty
and her heirs forever

the flag is hoisted.
Within the gesture

a signal lurks, a pluralism of the surface,
the monad fear, the parrot's feather,

contextualising the midnight revels
of fairies by fountain and forests-side,

the machine of emancipation. I say
he says he understands the question:

but what gender is this land?
Reconnaissance is protection.

In a glen white pigeons batter boughs with calamitous wings.
Immersed in fragrant nutmeg reflected in crystal streams.

Ten days' provisions remaining
though instilled with the blood

of two white pigeons we feel
confident of defending ourselves

against the natives. It's
a busy morning naming

as Choephoroe swing fantastic legs
in a grotesque fashion, laced in fragrant creepers.

Ardea Antigone or
Ardea Scolopacia

                              brought down
                              within the lyric.

What noble grounds for game!
        Rice and tea not satisfying

I discovered great sport
        beyond pandanus and bamboo.

The constant operation
        of (my) Westley Richards.

The reportage of shot
        as conscience affrays a narrative,

the shortest distance between
        two prepositions.

Red leader. Red leader. Red leader.
This is, as encircled it obliges

a refusal to accept bristling spears.
The warning shot. Queen's health.

Those we had already planted were doing well, and I hoped that this
benefaction might prove one of no small value,—perhaps to

Civilised man, or at least to the natives of the vicinity. Within
folly sketches are porphyry and basalt, as Jasmine like

for want of comparison, a carronade
of pleasure as supplies from Timor

are named as any other island,
and muskets whose locks

resist moisture. Captain Browse
bought 14 goats for a pair of old

pistols. By degrees all will fail
in the orienteering, palimpsest

-al segmentation in the
micropolitical space.

2.

Beauty is
singularly

persistent
in ascension, almost

in its provocation, the One
cannot be unconscious

of greens deeper than black,
anxiety and safety,

the elapse in repression
of a struggle and plurality,

the dark bow projecting
threateningly   above.

From precipice to precipice.
The rain swelling streams to torrents.

untouched yet ruined land broken
severe and yet beneath lofty pines
beauty dilutes the fear that makes all so
ugly

and though water so easily enters and passes
through, the sandstone resists us.
The natives for now
leave us unmolested

meat and flesh of the body
machine as Corporal Auger

inspires us all with hubristic strength:
taking a horse's burden on his back.

And so we reach
the elevated plain.

3.

Dried by parody, riverbeds
initiate comme une langue

in the semiosis of the hunt:
shadowing poise of past tense,

the stalked kangaroo or emu,
the spear patriotic in the forests

of New Hampshire, gravitas,
persistently,

though it's not New York
and nor is Buffalo.

Of course, they came in our absence.
Call and countercall across

the shallow valley.
So ambiguous to be

the call of some bird
or other creature.

200 men women boys
confronted on the hill brow

examine a pony. The gesture.
Like the kangaroo knocked down

and quickly back on its feet again.
Enchanted denizen, meta-black,

risen up, as if issuing forth
from each tree, each rock;

the forehead of their leader,
gleaming from this point of telling,

insinuated in this tension: a second shot
by entering his spear arm prevented reloading.

Coles has tangled the rifle in its cloth case, the other man falls to the cry O God! Sir, look at them, look at them. May the spear find its mark may its aim be true may its flight be swift. As my side is pierced they melt away into the forest, though emerge to take tenderly their fallen brother, I restrain the men from shooting, finding Necessity barely answerable for the first O so cruel obligation. My notebook gone, I sense the natives' dogs prowling nearby . . .

Monad particulars in the sun's rejoicing
a cloudless career, below the motifs

support the total recall of old growth forest,
explorative in the vascular spread

that brings only blockage
and necrosis. Finger on the trigger

the armaments doubling as ploughshares,
and despite the patronage of Lord Radstock

and improving agriculture an uncle
somewhere drinks his last drop,

or the bank forecloses.
From a monoplane the survey team

marks the limits of their spread.
The claim is buried beneath red tape.

The standard language
suppurates as lightning

scars sleep, and clamminess
feeds my wounds

as illustrations
colonise the page

and the coward
returns to the ship,

the minerals extracted
and the overseers

moving
further North:

Well, Sir, I'm sure if I were you,
I shouldn't think nothing at all
of having shot that there black
fellow: why, Sir, they're very
thick and plentiful up the
country. O Rushton of the Cape,
not to be reckoned with seri-
ously, your quaintness is a
comfort. Only seven or eight
miles separates from a great
fertility though on opening a
dead horse we find its belly
filled with sand from scraping
this thin pasture to the quick.

Art deco rim
sculpted filmically,

the vacant spaces
rich with trash,

the stylish emptiness
and the racketing

bankruptcy, yet
another expedition

Raleigh, eh?
And they say   Aphra Behn

was a bloke
      or a gorgon.

Passage Two

VICISSITUDES ON INTERIOR

1.

Direction merged in the comfortable hills,
navigational parataxis; who do you read through?

Bakhtin on the edges, the prospective
commerce driving us into the   painting.

This perspective a sheet of water
stumbled on by lost sheep as over

the ridges a magnificent river
drives forward like narrative

intrusion, or dysentery, the
porpoises up from the sea,

12 bark beds encircling a fire
as beneath pandanus the natives feed,

busy about the turtle oven,
iconic, like *mission civilisatrice*

The scale of barometric failure
in the othered peak, temperature

lowered with a gasp—guttural pressure,
rising smoke, the ache of old wounds,

the splendour of Prince Regent's River:
    verdant trepidation.

Deduction in the vacuum
as if the small bird

had learnt to breathe in nothing
and flourish,

bringing anxiety and not wonder
to the onlookers,

crowded against the surrounding
darkness.

Telescope: survey.
Enlarge the field: reduce

the gloomy shapes: shadows.
Vacuity: the tapered barrel.

The dog barks: child howls.
Humours pervade: solid air.

Breath circular: inhaled, the initial jolt
of life: we breathe

trepidation: interior
revolution: climate

predation: grain-eating mimic
engineers the plains: weirs;

here I: suggest
grain: the future.

Unmediated the discourse references
the luxuriant picture. Muddy on the fringes.

Confusing my powder pouch for another's
I am left weaponless, reliant on the others.

As the marsh gorges itself
on ponies, displacing anti-slime

in the three-d redness, the speaker's
authority is (made) vulnerable,

if not questioned. I would have it
as dialogue and it is up to me

to make myself understood.
It comes as no exaggeration:

The painted partrich lyes in every field
And for thy messe, is willing to be kill'd.

discourse of   storm
Lushington   body rot
a represented person   O
Lushington   who saw the
changing shape and fired   saw the musket ball enter
the body   instantly dead
Lushington   allegorical
blue cloth unfurling   serpent
entwining   small kangaroo
as   not a twig was
broken   not a rock was
turned   as the natives stepped
in one another's   neutral-ised
         footprints

Watershedding discourse double voiced
the parakeet and green ant (denizen

of sandstone), falling in with the
party   shrieeek   shrieeek

as we ascend on the
second attempt

establish a foothold
& descend to the swamp

without lyrical
sublimation

despite what
we'd like to think

were we outside
the illustration

2.

Between the country we leave and the country we enter
     the plot comes with the story
Between the country we leave and the country we enter
     we find the changing and adaptable sign
Between the country we leave and the country we enter
     the frill-necked lizard is a signal
Between the country we leave and the country we enter
     we waver, uncertain of style conventions
Between the country we leave and the country we enter
     parody links protocol and humour is forbidden
Between the country we leave and the country we enter
     wild oats, bearded like barley, are the soul of France
Between the country we leave and the country we enter
     a strange bird flies into view, swiftly, nameless

The understated sun touches tone,
prior to entering the cave, measuring distance
precisely, the roof a slab of sandstone, solid,
yet porous and allowing the steady flow, drainage
from the surface where cave is prehistory
and alien abduction incest,
as brother, I leave my wealth to the rust,
and their gesticulations as pure
renderings of visible speech, phonemic
rockpaintings, the sonority on non explicit action,
where simultaneity denies meaning and
is degraded into obviousness,
into the centrality of a dominant figure,
the enticing whispers of the mouthless

I have the party file through and experience
dominant tonic-cadence,
I sit and take notes, sketch;
Corporal Auger and I fall upon a momentous figure
carved in rock, the nose certainly Latin;
the natives shadow my steps
Lushington shoots a black cockatoo
I hunger for paintings: And revealed
curiously in this natural
chasm, the cave roof fissured
clothed in red, unreadable inscription
bands ringing his head
damp consuming, defacing
as if it too were uneasy in this foreign place

Interior—per—exotic—
outreach—repeating—
prospectively—a—desert—
or—a—sea—
and—getting—no—
closer—than—harsh—
contrasts—in—this—
mosaic—of—quotations—
tenuous—like—
a—Devil's—
Empire—built—
on—gunpowder—
and—rhythmic—
oscillation

Passage Three

1.

In search of a pass through ominous mountains Lushington and Walker set out with a party of men and horses. The horses were quickly spent. Twenty days' stores remain. My wound has split and Walker says I cannot continue at such a pace. I make regular astronomical and magnetic observations. The plain we cross has escaped the native conflagration, the kangaroos here are comparatively tame. Every member of the party gives an account of our journey, though most, I feel, exaggerate our exertions. In the global application of our project I consider whether there is room in the masculine flex of our language to incorporate the breath of women. It is true, that some of the men mention that if their mothers or wives were here they'd have something to say, but when they put this into words it sounds like parody, as if it is how they'd have them say it.

2.

Weather threatens
on the 29th Ultims

dogs consuming remnants of horses,
bones scatter

            wanton aggression
drops a dog where it stands

and returns to end
the tenuous life

of the last sheep
before descending

into the marsh, this genitalia
which could be drained

and turned prosperous,
this othering

It was his dog
        he owned that dog
it belonged to him
        he owned that dog
it followed his commands
        and it defended
his territory and he
        owned that dog,
it did as he commanded
        and was good insofar
as a dog could be good
        for him, lived up
to his expectations,
        he owned that dog,
it was his, despite the pack.

Rock mound tomb: scattered shell
plus added rocks suggesting

something spiritual,
the design not of these people

it takes five men two hours
to open and close like conscience;

localism in the epiphany,
the sideward glance

in this aid to conversation,
the comfort of interiors

post-expedition,
as I lend my horse

to a sick Mustard
and suffer for my kindness.

Cross-bearing dialect
where no name can enter

this lexicon, the flex
of the mother tongue,

as would have this land
as would have this dead horse

ossified as a meeting place
or place of triumph, like

cross-swords in an atlas
of conquest and collapse

that is simultaneously
plaintive   moral   recreative

in the ecologic compass,
dialogue of terra incognita

schematic overlay of the bright
realism, the x-ray fauna

internalising the radiation,
thick shells of bark

really the walls of a humpy
not far from Hyde Park,

Christopher Smart poised
unremittingly on the walls

of the ambassador's house,
all of that wasted central space

just gloating, like sociability,
and the gesture that supports

itself on plonk from
the Barossa valley

such good quality, even
in the warm grip of

the centrally-heated Old World,
as we discover the natives

have in fact left the food stocks
un-damaged,

that only the horse
left tethered

has perished, as we retrace
our steps and break

into cheers on the support vessel
answering our guns

like the press,
the eager guests.

Horses. Eleven damaged ponies
that would be valueless if brought to sale.

It's not worth loading them back onto ship.
We turn them loose such that they

have the chance of becoming the progenitors
of a numerous herd.

                    The garden I planted
shall disappear: the luxuriant pumpkin vine,

the breadfruit and cocoa nut,
sink into the sombre trees.

Unsupported by social utterance
the garden is a valueless

disconnected domain
of field notes.

Epilogue

After all is
said and done

I will sit back
and gloat

I mean, I will
be able to say

on the
authority

of Mr
Gould

that the fe-male
kangaroo

I shot
was

of a whole
new species.

The Martiniquian revolutionary theorist Frantz Fanon, the Ethiopian-American film-maker Haile Gerima, and the Palestinian-American cultural critic Edward Said have all registered the impact of Tarzan on their impressionable young selves. Gerima recalls the "crisis of identity" provoked in an Ethiopian child applauding Johnny Weismuller as he cleansed the "dark continent" of its inhabitants: "Whenever Africans sneaked up behind Tarzan, we would scream our heads off, trying to warn him that "they" were coming." Ella Shohat and Robert Stam, Global/Local ed. Rob Wilson and Wimal Dissanayaike DukeUniversityPress 1996

The other
families

of this part
of the earth

have been
little studied;

the *Papuan* family
of New Guinea

and ad-
jacent islands,

and the
Australian

langu-
ages.

(Bloomfield, *Language*)

manbound parakeet rat-stripped to the bone
deadly dead man wild or domesticated
as trees smoke and opossums perish
and the bandicoot is ripped from its lair
conceptually in the glades of Central Park,
black hole of the skating rink, Frederick
Lar Olmsted decisively as Hallet Nature
Sanctuary's bull paradise beauty quicker
stopping lines for birds transpires like a
charming ride in a gloomy countryside,
for he came down from Venice by invitation
and colonised parallel space, points of contact
potential like paint soaking through from an
original: the now the then the potential

northern variety stronger than its southern
brother as the stand is taken, perfect specimen
desensitized schematic as nodal glands,
as per expediency in the obtaining,
like glasshouses and zoos and follies
crowding out the engineering feats
of the century, that under proper
treatment they might be raised
very considerably in the scales
of civilization, as the data
of benefaction is the seasonal
blood flowing through the Trepang
Malay King, the near civilized
answer: that earthen pot, the shard heap

a blainey is a hot wind of the east that blows
out of a white edifice that may look like a library
or centre of learning but is in fact a publicity
office for the national front; a hanson is an
unsteady wind from the north that incites
television poles to reveal their true in-
clinations, that dressed up as freedom
of speech snides and chips at the old block,
burns that fat around the wood-chop
of the camp fires, yarns like barbed wire
with every divorce and blames everybody
but Mr Usberres and his European
turn of shoulder, body and legs
being better proportioned in a league of nation

Though thirsting for an immediate return
I heed advice to rest, to discuss my aims

and prospects with Governor Stirling,
to prepare for another expedition

to the rim of the Interior,
to bless it profitable

in the name of Her Majesty,
to proclaim the dominions

of Chance and Integrity,
to carry the scales of justice

over the grotesque body of savagery
to enact its becoming

to donate its skeleton
to the Royal College of Surgeons

Graphology (prototype)

Graphology: Canto 1

handwriting resonates
like the voice: larynx's
scrawl calibrating

the signature
or oft mentioned cal-
ligraphy: the cliché

becomes identity
in the autograph, the book
as well fetishized

becomes the programme
we mark as strokes
in the book of hours,

those amateur graph-
ologists from Suetonius
to Poe legal & validated

by time, which fades
like a secret signature,
or—unearthed

like palimpsest—
predecides beneath
the text or texts

mentioned in parallel
texts fingerprinting as object
in the visualizations

of personality
like the neutral Swiss
taking a great interest

in the addresses
on other people's
letters as traits

ethnographicize
the characterology
of empirical schools

against the fear
of pathology, elemental
in the barometer

of repetitions
in the machine printed
image that allows

only the signature's space
but this IS the age. Degenerating
the unconnected writing

as theory angles
& forms against curves
of food production,

the specialist items
labelled brightly
in the specialist shops:

the upstrokes vigorous
amongst the arrhythmic,
as the nihilists delete

the superfluous,
the detailed attention
& vital opposing of discipline:

that you don't need
an atom smasher & can do it
at home, amateurism

bringing the charlatans
loud against empiricism,
the essentialists

apologizing
as the Marxists
rule straight demo-graphic

lines and print
the written, the ornaments
in Hitler's signature

DO look like
his moustache,
& identical uniovular

twin brothers
produce similar script
with small variations:

the loops & pressure,
end & horizontal strokes
differing slightly

as technology squeezes
out the guts of the twentieth
century: the forgery's

trembling line
the shadow amidst
data: who's who

dressed in the same
fashion, vogue
in the hat's tilt

& an admirer's
or detractor's
description, or sub-

scription to trends
in the attainment of identity:
they might have different

fingerprints—whorls
& loops & arches—
but still come from

Perth and live
in the same pore
of the social

organism.
They say he writes
with two distinct hands

though thematically
there is common ground
if the script can be

translated, the spacing
clear minded
if irregular

as if to disguise
contradictions
which suggest

[272]

to certain critics
a lack of knowledge.
The mechanical skill

of the Victorian cursive
as the moon full & deliberate
flourishes amongst the tide-

riven ripples of the river.
Could it be said, despite
the fluid surface,

it writes with a determined
if shaky hand (?) this stout
image: varying

with its cycle
& the weather
& the climate

& any number
of phenomena WE
can perceive

but cannot
put name to?
Forgery or disguise

or mnemonic codings
that are the character-
ology, that rather

we may not want
to imprison by recognition
but recall for en-

lightenment. As the sand
scrawled by the wind
is blanked by a downpour

or the crystallography
of salt flourishes
despite the deed of title

an obituary witnessed
by the bank as it closes
the mortgage

on an unproductive
property on the edge
of the wheatbelt

where language is worth-
less without rain,
the ambidextrous scribblings

of water. Body of water.
Unwritten the characterized
fleshly interest expressed

as the blood
as symmetry
as co-ordinations

to mark as standard,
the model against which
all measurings

are conducted, the measure
kept in vaults, exact-ness
allowing ramblings

& ponderous
deliberations
of bureaucracy.

Graphology: Canto 2

In the crypto signal corps
big business scrutinizes
the script, this suppression

of the lyric, these conspiracies
of Babel, this "but Engels
wrote the good bits anyway"

lens through which
Beauchataud's free features
occupy outside the apparent

message, releases that plosive
in the aggro cross bar
that t's attentively

subjective rush
to be heard above the platitudes
or ingratiating

pleas: ah, such
an exact and synthesistic
science!

like a back issue of *Time*
or a note from Governor
Macquarie, the mark

on the colophon
of a Prynne edition
that's not a condescension

to the art of printing, rescued
or dragged sullen
from the loft, imprest,

impresa, impression
like a night-scope
of the neglected situation

or a heat-sensitive
out-of-print Irish poet,
a friend of Yeats

who could only
sign the fly leaf, the volume
such a holy object;

graphological
exegesis carries
the disclaimer

in the *grand guignol*
of pictures, like diplomacy
within the image

varied in-micro,
every twitch of Bismarck's
guile and ferrous nature;

as formniveau
is underwritten
by the rhythm

of variations in
pronunciation:
Ludwig Klages'

Handwriting and Character,
and later Max Pulver
preoccupied by the world space

of a sheet of gleaming
white paper, deeply
infernal the transcoded

descent of Virgil, as in
the undotted-i
of his sepulchral title

the "sin of omission"
accounts for poetry's
repetitions as negligence

is not the shifting
of the painting, as per
Lofty Nabarrayal Nadjamerrek

Deadman c1968
Mann River Plateau,
Western Arnhem Land,

natural pigments
on eucalypt bark,
as symbols lose themselves

to entanglement
the barometer of strength,
those incidents of assessment,

that aspirations to express
vanity, pride, dynamism,
and, above all else: enthusiasm

Graphology: Canto 3

altruistically
the forger considers
the hungry readership,

that death should have
curtailed the gift,
the output;

to plagiarise is to eulogise
he said, but I don't dream
in your script so how

can you write me?
mistletoe like a concentration
of crop marks, abandoned

in the *trompe l'oeil*
of the vacant,
the wind-scarified tree

the recovered text
a dialectic of greed,
evocation of the lyric

like Archimedes' principle,
as the hyper-lyrical removes
all thoughts of death,

which is a tyranny anyway
and of dubious authenticity:
doubtful authorship

originality
ingenuity
value

the phrenologist reads
that organ of veneration
as Charlotte Brontë

would have him do: a dip where
his organ of veneration
should have been: the

signature of God so altered;
exteriorization in the enjambed
word-units: as the script

flows away from its starting point
& Pulver hesitates on a point
of recollection, and defiantly

writes against a sudden fear of heights
or seeing his pet cat hit by a car
alters the slant of his letters;

the sinister move to the left:
the un-positive movement
against right-left reading

of text, reversed arcades
delicately negotiated,
though to what end:

the post-colonial subversion,
the page deflecting,
a Manichaean reflex

against the darkness
of the imprint,
the aspect of words

as aspects of time,
calibrations of the linear
in an occupied zone

that mimics space,
substitutes for conscience:
part of the eternal

Western
trans-
creation

it takes wave on wave
of newness, of resolve,
of auto-garlandism

in the Movement,
to confirm the tenacity
and intactness of the

transported culture, its ability
to adapt and prosper
and absorb the mirrored

migrations, to build upwards
and economise the aspirations
of the estate, to ward off the hunger

for sprawl, to find new places
on the factory floor for unskilled
labourers, despite newsprint plants

erupting malignantly in Wapping,
or at Herdsman Lake,
like Colma, the US City of Souls,

a vast necropolis making space
available in zones of occupation,
like Lacan's "cipher of his

mortal destiny", like Dame Margot
Fonteyn signing your mother's
paper napkin in a Perth restaurant,

her flourishing hand
working against the limitations
of the surface,

as delicate
as the avant-garde
is not.

Graphology: Canto 4

The handwritten auto-
hagiography, the Samuel Pepys
trivialities, collective

self-adulations dressed up
as items on a shopping list,
movements in early

twentieth-century
European art: what of
Christopher Brennan?—

whose symbolist obsessions
sent poetry in Australia
after the 1968 uprising

hurtling off in a different
direction, fifty-five years
after his magnum opus,

as Artaud maintains
the definitively mad
confront the mad of history,

or so claimed,
for history is simply
an appraisal of the likely,

as trinkets in the galleries
of the British Museum
plunge downwards

into materialism: though
annotations on the decorative
subdue the cataclysmic moods

of the war correspondent,
bring remorse, potassium bromide
in the Garden of Norman Lindsay,

vital sexist in the welter
of crossings, the Greeks
being the incorp-

orators of philosophy,
in the brilliant hand that could
be a simulation,

a computer-generated
construct: the ink
blotting on the wartime paper.

Damn those charlatan
oneiromancers, dredging
the semi-epistemological sleep

of archetypes, the staves
of possibility, the effusions
of obstructed exposures,

conglomerates of stratas,
as they institute the analysis,
the traits of the us in the

disjunctive pronoun,
the subject diagnosis
as one's own children

would be taught [early on]
not to grip the pen
like that.

Graphology: Canto 5

"You see these big letters? I am now writing to you in my own hand."
GALATIANS 6:11

she hand-wrote poems
even though the power
had not failed;

the precise space occupied
by each letter represented
a parcel of breath;

in the absence of a
typewriter each letter
was located in a single

unit on the graph paper,
binaries punctuating
the background noise,

the radio telescopes
scanning the variations
of an ink-black sky;

the consistent interruption
like Klages' graphic pulse
not the atomic clock's

precise rendering
of the character,
laid bare before

the amateur
composer of bagatelles—
trivial offerings blown up

like evidence
in a murder trial,
like the hieroglyphics

demotic characters,
and Greek of the
Rosetta stone;

and this written
for assemblage
in a rhizome-book;

it is the absent
Nomadology that
should have been

unrooted in the
Making of A Homeland,
as the thirty-five year old Morris

is driven along
the country laneways
on a brilliant Summer's day,

the interior smelling
slightly musty though not
fuming noxiously like

interiors fresh
from contemporary
factories;

the tooled vinyl
evokes the odour
of a Chevrolet flat-top

in the Avon valley,
South Western Australia,
the post-Mabo lysis

strung up in the courts,
the racist graffiti
on the Kelmscott bus stops

the diminishing exteriorization,
as dimensions decrease in the hastily
applied scrawl; moving inland

substantial horizontal
movements of air
morph sand paintings

while snakes twitch
on the hot, fluid fields
of silica.

Graphology: Canto 6

The Victorian Cursive
underwrites the generational
counterpoint, as on Jesus Green

a new kind of printing is learnt,
the sans serif of the centre,
the clean roads between the pale

blue lines of flatland horizons,
the fens darkly coming to life
like underworld commons,

dumped cars and evidence
too hot to be stored in the basement
settling into strata of lies:

it is natural the Englishman
should turn to Chinese characters,
watching the amateur punter

being tricked by the mud,
a somnolent sun still reeking
of Chernobyl, the mushrooms

sensitive to his
public misgivings
sub rebus echoes

from the formula,
the name I sign is mine
iste ego sum,

and property is the registration
of an item as no two marks
are the same, despite

a generational deviation
from value, the price
for having more robust

strains of wheat, the defeat
of rodents in the long white bins
that in the distance—also

flat—they curve over the
horizon as a rapport is signalled
with the controller

of a potentially massive market,
the prospects of clear
communication

enhance the possibilities
for reward: at school my handwriting
was a damning indictment

of fluctuating genes.
The book donated in
and to the chapel

had been signed, the
transcription
a reminder of the

flesh's weakness?
In the same way
you might become a minister

of divinity, ecumenically
describing a course
through printed liturgies.

Graphology: Canto 7

What use if we can't
note some of Dante
in his epic diva comics,

climb down a few rungs
of his sorry internal workings,
extricate around the footnotes

like revivals, enthusiastic
resurrections
of the *roman à clef*?

as through draft on draft
the distance grows
like counter-revolution

and paranoia rises
in(to) the publisher's stable,
threatening to bolt

the door of learning
as if the inscription
on the lintel

said welcome
to my nightmare;
no erratum

will erase
the faulty character,
a nasty business

this considering best
how your light may be spent,
as naffy dressing

is like Henry Fleming
raising the flag
after doing a runner;

or holding centre stage
when the visitors' book
he omitted to sign

is held open
for the crowd's vigorous
applause: it's the setting

that counts as the black crayon
is cut by the stylus, revealing
the deep red of the original coating.

Graphology: Canto 8

eczema and asthma
express in different locales;
papyrus or parchment

predating illumination,
in the manner driven
narratives

the <u>masses</u> cannot read
this constant process
of encrypting (the graph):

literacy is purely
relative and will inform
industriously—

in the savagery of downstrokes
those given the key to crack the codes
dredge the primal sludge for error.

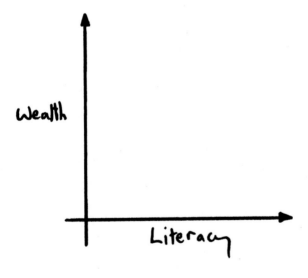

Graphology: Canto 9

The furious disgrace;
athadeia and megaloprepia,
eventually a stoush

behind the pub, Dikê
like a running shoe
imprinted on your forehead,

like authenticity
making even the scurrilous
legit., as if verification

makes it more inclined
to elucidate the truth,
in *tableau vivant*

the decaying bonds
of molecular discourse
are the *cause célèbre*

enjambed against
the common good,
like Hobbe's maintaining

metaphor is never
understanding
in the libretto

of cognition: half perceived
the semi-vegetation
lifted above the town

on the only hill for miles:
"half risen in its sullen bloom"
is not the data needed

to compile the simulation,
while she who admired
learns to hate the author

as the tinctured evening
is painted solid:
what's left of the sensation

when you are thinking hard
and feeling intuitive? the label
on the back of the photograph

reverses through; and now
the id is positive
it's reached its telos,

converted in history,
that patented meshing
of non sequiturs.

Graphology: Canto 10

the sky-written greeting
you recall from childhood,
the satellite projecting

Coca Cola ~~from satellites~~
like an allegory for divine
intervention but it's

as obvious as pop art
and merely reflective
of money and the rapid

emergence of gender
sexuality, which didn't
exist before the twentieth

century de-spite Marx
and the nineteenth's
arousals of the clitoris

as a thing-in-itself.
The post-script
ex-tends as hypotactic

syn - tax
logically & metrically
contrasting

with the paraphrased
compositional hypo-products
of the New Lyricism

in a field where
dis-engaged ploughs
will not engage

or share
even the tenuous
topsoil —

unable
in times of draught
to free

the left margin
of the field,
to strike out

across
the dusty paddocks
where

the possibility
of moisture
declares itself.

Sheep Dip

The hand-writing is recognisably his
though deterioration is obvious.

The rage is in the agricultural
absence off the oik and redneck
blustering with feigned indifference
as the sun explodes and deflates

this sunset reckoned
spectacular, the trash
of an outer vocabulary
for where it's tough

there's no locale and leisure
only drives against its place
which is why nature has to be
forced back on to itself; the crazy

raddling is furious and takes it out
on those nearabouts, inside
it's linear but without,
they tread on egg shells

or hang on tenterhooks
like the madly butchered meat
offcut and tenderised
by pounding against the collective

vegetarian face of the altering
markets, they say you can
no longer read yourself, narratology
skewed as if the church warden is everything

and knows better in a gendered district,
from school to work
when there's a bloody harvest
to be brought in and the skies all baled up

and glowering, and you call
that pretty, as if you'd paint
the fucking thing, as if a brothel keeper
inside my head should take shorthand

        or tally the movements up and down
        the ramps, a leg stuck out
        in the three-tiered truck
        as it goes south to ships,

killed properly in the head
that's prepared to dine
accordingly, a stinking etiquette
that has me declared a bigot

        in the broadcasted rant
        as if the chapel were all that'd
        got in this far and been tossed out
        at that. Let them tell their stories.

I feel that water coursing below your feet
caustic and threatening to burst
up and out over the putrefaction green
of the fields, where the sheep aren't crammed in

because the space aches and there's a hole
overhead that goes right through to space
it cries to make me meditate
and I can't remember the last time

I expressed this hate like an abscess
on my registration, an inking well
on my birth certificate. But still
I speak and clearly enunciate

my total hate, the rank stands
of tanning trees, the protected species
paddling in the dam, the demarcations
between the giddy crops

and firebreaks. Which is the Karma
of being stranded on an island
that's bigger than the ocean
it wallows in, and you're trying

to read your future in the tepid
entrails of sheep that seem to be
of normal size despite their owners
being as large as bloody giants,

and one-eyed. To drive beyond the eye
and see the corporate beast thrash about,
crushing your neighbours as one by one
the deadline falls on their pathetic

overdrafts, the Calvinistic
inevitability of drought.
As the times change I change with them.
If you can't read it then you're stuck

back there and I'll go under
faster than a fucking lump of granite.
The beer-dark haze of the heat-shimmer
on the endless outback roads,

the roadhouse oasis
where truckies pick up hitch-hikers
to take them out like sheep
under the dirty great cavernous sky.

Those stifling breezes the farts of giants.
The trophies of my triumph
read loudly in the Book of Yields,
and the ploughing reveals

a disk or tine from my father's
time—and he went blind
and never wrote his name.
His mark was a blot on the family tree,

a dull and stringy eucalypt.
And as the weeds arose out of the crop
it reigned down organo-phosphates
as the labels predicted. From Delphi

to Dandaragan the heady tribes
of printed matter settled
residually, heavier than soil.
And in the veins occluded

like a blockage around which tissue
became less friable. The tillage
of identity, to burst a vessel
in the contracting space: it looks

bigger than it really is, this
minutia in the epic. The fraternity
leaves it out and drunkenly
accepts the shortcomings,

staggering about the hills,
dancing on volcanic wastelands,
that without qualities
I seek to bind my indifference's

in the shallow pans, the tremors
rippling through the paddocks
like conquest, as if cock-a-hoop
you think you've got the better

of survival and named this place
The Shakes as if it's been as easy
to recall as nostalgic rock & roll;
Tellaird limp despite the centrefold

had never practised as a youth
on unattractive ladies, a tendency
to reflect, to look back and consider
home was not such a bad place

after all. Regret as outburst:
the script driving windward
despite the shifting of the timbers,
the barn that went down

in the tumult.
The powerlines sputtering
about the town-site,
the sibilance of light.

they wouldn't recognise me now—
touched by heat and sirens
ringing through the main street
the foul beaked and ranked clawed

birds that I blast with my semi-auto,
weeping as the feathers
shower down like leaves
disconnected by Autumn;

null & void, withdrawn
behind the labels, drumming up
angularity & cramped as alter ego,
fuming in the first person narrative

like balls of Berlin Wool
in the letter to a close companion,
the neglected form
blamed upon the writing tool

his posture was increasingly feminine
though he raged and exposed his genitals
to show his trembling
implement

                as if his body were sketched
                whilst crossing
                the roughest stretch
                of ground;

the correcting applications
embellishing the zone, touching up
the outbursts and collapses
with a stumbled gesture

                behind the eight ball;
                that is now will never come
                and has never been as anger passes
                nondescript

the beasts—verminless—
dripping in the sun's brilliant
paddocks: helios descending
blacker than a retrospective night.

—

Annotations

Annotations

Imperfect memory
has chasms deeply yawning
in reception, in Rossby

waves rip up
the Northern light,
authentically driven

like song in Virgil's
ninth eclogue, unable
to prevent the soldiery

claiming territory,
goats steady on the path
as a noonday sun

'

is guessed overhead,
sky like mirrored sea
somewhere outside

the concept, specified
as nought on a Beaufort scale—
resistance of city

enticing the veritable
with imitations, odes
outflanking balladry

and the strongest
surviving a publicity
of false announcements,

death certificates
reaping an overwhelming
narrative voice,

the gleaning poet
wasting chaff,
winnowing

applications
of folly, of hydraulics
and terraces.   Frost

harnesses
mid-winter days
and glass houses

glower, while brooding
off-season a cat's-paw settles
in the sulky waters

of vacations—
kindled like bounties
itemized as recollection

despite weather's
patterned changing,
or the Trotskyite

throwing a spanner in the works,
privileged protest,
viewer-friendly

movement, eco-gendered
and specific,
plausible selves

languishing in a cell
as if caring only
for biography,

tin cans stressing criteria,
spray paint deepening as visibility drops
and Beaufort is a file

held in Bangkok,
an absurdist drama
just outside a realm

of Hansard, hydro-
logical cycle, or circular
of phlegms and humors,

zones where particles
are never smaller than atoms,
and capacity

for consistency
is Aristotelian in its
magnitude

and breadth;
a flurry driving the stuff
of a burst flour bag

over a small town,
its only industry,
Bing Crosby in Dongara

Western Australia,
some time outside his own,
spatially readjusted

in the prospect
of Song's Cycle,
that Menalcas himself

had an indigenous
turn of phrase, cultish
in the master territory,

sending flares up
over pacified waters
and costing millions

in wanton search projects,
fire-stick
burnt as anti-eco

propaganda
by smart asses hungry
in the politburos

of down under,
that we might call this
analogous

and diachronically
Australian: moving in or out
from a centre,

red rock contra-band
in the traveller's tale,
horizontal

conquest, Mont Blanc
of an unsublime nothingness,
the pun they might later

name as Voss: dingo
credited as wolf, incest
passed off as suppression

or continental drift,
precipitating in tongues
voiced like nulla nullas,

and sulphur-coated authors
appropriating steady print,
emphasizing vicarious

sandpaintings
emblematic totalizing missions
of justice,

quivering stretched below
oak primeval in the empire's
hulks and brigs,

leaning to the wind
as seas of wheat ripple
and find calibration,

ideolectically
damning a sunning
lizard, peripheral

and itemized
late in the piece,
stabilizing

yet another chunk
of bourgeois text
liberating constructions

of time tracked
as if technology is prognostic
and curving like swathes

of the monitor's tail
outside the boundaries
of instinct, distinctly

intense on the shores
of an inland sea, lugged vessel
lost to sudden storm,

the faint echo of hubris
barely bothering to lend its name
to such irrelevant

activities, at this point
in time, though inconsistency
lavishes growth and irrigates

doubt self-reflexively,
in under and over tone
per source of vibration

per pure tone
and vibrancy
thresh-holding the peripheral crops

primed with super phosphate
draining through sand plain
and percolating. Ground

water devaluing
the filling magnet,
sundial pulling

the sphere concurrently,
gliding vowels
as exclamation

rests above
and the sun lies
weather shift in skies

plural and elided,
condensed as script
as high density

fields compressed
behaviourist drilling
tines occluding

nudged furrows
in observed vents
goldenly cleaving

against silo walls,
idiomatic anti-contrast
formalising plough discs

and intensifying,
when with hanging
fog smoke rises

vertically,
rain following
Inwards' lore

as a warble lodges
in the syrinx
and a gift of pipes

is accepted
in another tongue,
sung hand-in-hand

down to the scrawl,
the Miltonic hand
inscribing molecular bonds:

[316]

Poggioli's homo artifex
restless in the crowd,
chaining itself to trees

destined for the saw,
pristine interiors
voiced velar plosive

qua prescriptive pulp
and digestion, fallen
forms reduce the growing,

passé simple, solid
contracts in groves
of influence,

a boustrophedonic
atlas inscribed
in an insular hand,

withholding field bins
against moisture,
abundant risk

of docking
at the sample hut,
the asshole's chirography

both fancy and quick,
flattened on a threshing floor
of weights and quality

and madrigals of cogs and fencing
wire entangling hungry sheep
introduced and straining

despite the constant
slaughter, gallows
frantic beneath an amber

metonymy.
Iron age forts—
flat and hollow

as rings of hills
are not—solid
to a granite core,

solid accents embedded
and sexualising
the strongest warheads

remaining after
disarmament: in Darwin
yellow cake hovers

and Wharfies
equivocate,
white singlets glowing

lawn mowers coughing
coagulated oil
over Southern pastures

[318]

and board rooms
of generalization,
the stereotypical industry

chiding hurt given
by a slight to a stalwart
acceptably different

and sticking his or her neck out
for a brother or a sister,
for smooth verse and an unlettered

muse, but not a brandname.
Unlettered nature pshaws
the High Table suit

as the gong is rung
and a vegan is catered for
without obvious fuss:

unlettered nature pshaws
annotation as decoration
on cake compares

with ploughing out fields,
desert closing in and in and in,
roused strictly against

a bordering comedy,
distinctly white torrents
of herbicidal foam

within the parallel framework,
circuits of nostalgia replete
in dawning, light enhancing

the manager's boyish eyes
as hunters claim to have preserved
that species from extinction.

A Gotham City decay
pneumatic on a platform
of seedling trays

donated by the ministry
hawking tickets in sound
gardens, sunning

ethnic allocation
as intimate with profit
and profligacy

joined in holy manifestoes
in new countries,
overlaying,

palimpsesting
and re-creating
myths of origin

to account
for missing books
and dampen the sound

of oratory; art deco
like stations of a neglected
cross that could

name names if subpoenaed,
restless with a city's litigation,
closing optimism

by the agency
and counterbalancing
rival claims as they work

to diminish sovereignty
or rearrange Niagara falls
as units of drainage

or philanthropy,
artificial lakes bobbing up
like satellites

in contradictory orbits,
tossed corpses risen
on gas beds,

defrosting apathy
and the town electing
a new mayor.

Collective action
threatens to save
a wild life sanctuary

and foxes are busy
gnawing away at the wildlife,
as if they had some other

place to go
and are being down right malicious,
as in, you know, they rip

the heads of chickens
just for the hell of it,
observing codes of unknowing

like repetition—
you can bet your bottom
dollar on it

in any currency
or jargon of insecurity—
no Trojan horse threatening

to undermine evaluation
as action in-itself,
this cult of courtesy.

Distrust profoundly this I
the autograph hunter employs
as sample or prompt,

as worth n/a's its awe,
as lock stock and barrel
and ankh and crucifix

are honestly exploited
as fictions and I allows
the God in self

free expression,
questioning hybridity
on the fringes of modernity,

like white-walled wheels
leaving burn-out marks
on the road stretching

all the way
to liberation theology,
overcast and dry

as lightning strokes
a distant coast
and I sweats

under boughs
of corrugated iron
mimicking flight delays

in spaces growing less stable
with each diminishing front,
the tiny compass in the sole

of your shoe leading
it astray. Machine op-
erators cling like

testosterone
whirled out of
the dynamo

where horizon
is a manipulation
of shadow and electricity

and the elegy
is the profoundest ex-
pression of love,

an exceptional network
of otherness
and referentiality:

the facts
dragging snow
off the lake

as more than method
effects gaps in whiteness,
a production-line mausoleum

regionally enacting
where I becomes they and we
and rolls off;

as labour divides
componentry
in a discourse

of exclusion
fringe
communicates

with fringe,
let us know
about it.

Because the you has moved
calque undulates about a scene
reminiscent

of a home run
hit in a big game
by a team whose town

is on the brink
of bankruptcy.
And tourists

won't care and don't
and won't go where
a trophy dislodges poverty

in a grand room
that is treeless and without
tracts of water,

bitter birds
kerning tunes
on fence posts,

generic fumblings
itemizing
change rooms.

The power-lifted soil
supports bloated granules
of succession,

each weed uttering
monopolies of stanzas,
hedgerows cut back

as copse planters
head out against a sharp cold,
deflecting rotation

and insisting,
radarscopic blanking
enforcing fallowness,

direction
as progressive
as depth

in the play of light,
a surface current
playing up like popularity

ridging-in over
high art, a Theocritan
portraiture

indicating position
with precision, the tractor
clumping lugs of clay

in rotations
sublimating
the craved for object,

atmospheric
machine propagating
subaltern speech

(Homi Bhabha c/- Gareth Griffiths)
maintaining the for
in it's in-between

an edictness of English,
a first crop's struggle
expectedly on Walden Pond

uncertain, assaulting
darkly the rudest places,
those dark unruly spaces

surfacing the carapace
of earth, busy
in strengthening

strain
and the comfort
of parchment.

Facts indulge such
as Yakabindie Bob
paying almost nothing

for the labourings
of indigenes,
tribal women

currency
against the binaries
of wool and starvation,

the prevalence of
of and the
in the pastoral quiddity:

a hard time of it was had
beneath the oral tree,
as story ran into story

under the clauses
of speech event,
the curing ritual.

A storm rolls in
tithing angular blooms
out of dirt,

red dust runs as wine
over the front pages
of a local rag,

and celebration
is named as corroboration
or uprising.

Pressure Suite Tilde

Pressure suit tilde notation

impressing atmosphere
clamping & compressing
& breaking through at the points
of weaker science, tilde floating
wantonly as stress over
technical language, the tribal
drumming on the skin,
the collapsing auditory verve
as the sounds of discovery
break through, synaesthetic
on the canopy, the helmet's
imperial visor: too deep
this conquest, this groping
for air, the sound it makes

Influences

That profound machine
        unturns the lathed leftocracy
like personality, a comparison
        sang froid anagrams
of bitterness & disappointment,
        once best friends parrying,
dispensing the jabs, failing
        to recognise they've been hit
& are hitting themselves;
        or quorums that didn't
quite come off, or branch-stacking
        failing to give the campaign
the glow they'd like; & as
        influence is about shape
cosmetics mask the covert
        body: from him I take
& am taken by her, but refuse
        to acknowledge it in
a public place. The journo's
        congratulations fail
to worry your conscience
        & so you are caught. Yes,
I stay here out of allegiance,
        but also gratitude, & pleasure.

Marginalia

"Smooth verse, inspired by no unlettered Muse..."
The Excursion, WILLIAM WORDSWORTH

Unlettered nature
pshaws the annotation
roused up and bordering
distinctly white torrents

A series of parallel
circuits lights up
in the boy's eyes

Scene from above,
the sands of
the hour glass

Textual reruns
whose crimes
flaw us;

Hah! Likely
story—existing
without quote marks,

Soft effects.

[335]

"The rancid power of the continuum"

If sleep is a slurry of rapid eye movement
or out and out negation of time, the stairs
take us nowhere—and "like" as comparison
becomes the test-firing of fireworks three nights
before Guy Fawkes (I won't be here). Here
is memory a transparent cell, a typo
everybody's trying to fix, as one's best lines
are transcribed and the author's hand
is an illegible correction; what was it
the woman from Tatler was saying about
Heidegger, a sister? Making room
for his misdemeanours. Xenophobia—
please explain?—is not the machine
imposing continental drift, the whites
of the eyes legislated and glowing,
like the rewriting of rewritten history.

Breathers

for John Ashbery

The new world's breathers simulate an attic vase—
hoplites red-lining against the public hum, kicking
      up their heels as shields almost overlapping
take the wrap, a fashion show beneath the glow
of a hustling city vicarious as the weirs open & close,
open & close, as if the locks of some minor river
      meandering inland might offload its traffic,
counter sidereal the choking graphics of the charts,
      all higher than the pleasant banks of grass,
trinkets of community busy in adulterating arts,
graceful in robes of ancient sailcloth, the designer
insisting on simplicity and sweet neglect as below
      the crowds scramble to meet their
debts, their need for breath and the artist's trick

Honest, Theocritus!

for John Ashbery

Interphase, cross-over, fringe exchange,
collusion or conversion, absorption or rejection,
counterpoint over peat beds and spreads
of chalk, or sandy perimeters that run with the wind
or collude with pads of concrete marked out
in fields of neglected sheep and decrepit horses,
the RSPCA rolling past daily, building up their case
against an eccentric who won't leave the house
to look after her charges—contractors
moving closer and closer with a circular utterance
as if the Song of Solomon were pure pastoral,
as if resolution did not compare itself to a steel trap,
the mind of the songster busy as a bee on the outskirts
of redress, where summer sits in lush shade—gravitas
of fossil fuel hanging close about, issuing wreaths
to naked Fellows who might invade King's College Chapel
to act out some drunken rite they call Sentimental
Gesture to a Great Tradition, a recasting of progress!
Might be a photo somewhere—honest, Theocritus!

Stain or Resonance in The Curve: A Hymn
for Louis Armand

> "*Here: where, then?* 'Voice of no one, once more.'"
> MAURICE BLANCHOT

Replica Bounty reverses and pivots
like a beacon to the wor(l)d, a minor gift
welling below the rush of a chopper
heading out towards The Heads, the curve
of The Bridge as ironic as grace replicating
movement of a bird or body arching
into sensuality, pleasant disaster,
fingernail parings not-quite dramatic
in the "primitive" stain that some call guilt,
relaxing on their verandahs without a neighbour
in sight, (distantly a hum suggests
the presence of an ultra-light).
The flags flutter, subverting a Southerly
Buster, becoming as nationalistic as prizes
and as subjective as acceptance speeches,
and that neat piece of architecture
imperious on the point over there, built
with a hell-of-a-lot of lottery money.
A tourist calibrates as a toaster-like
building pops up—ugliness so close
to the Harbour's other jewel! The amniotic
waters swirl about the pylons and wealth
is a cruiser or a particularly
well-hung yacht. Those delicate shells,
so gendered in the afterglow of the 60s,
the vicissitudes of a slashed ribbon,
the Cossington-Smith advertisement,
the germ in the language of water.
The Golden Grove and Scarborough split
and curve away from each other
on their green hulls. The light
doesn't do very much. A chilled moon

breathing for an entire afternoon
distresses blue, and music
is the husbandry of cars arcing
volume—it's just a dialect of noise
and tollgates click with coins—YOU
haven't lived if the crossing hasn't been made—
there & back—at least once in your life.
So you're a hostage. You'd like
to have confidence in place, in history.
The buzz of The Rocks countercultures
slick resonance of presence: those
indigenous utterances, those percentage points
on the national register pinned
down by apartment blocks, the ana-weight
of traffic keeping the curve squeezed
between two unbending points, discobulus
in the woomera, the satellite navigation
equipment carrying a party out-of-this-world,
the Sydney Olympics as fast as the millennium,
techno-sharp, opportune, and eco-friendly.

Naff or Language signifiers are fucking boring
(lyric overlay for Beastie Boys number)

aka typos mutatis mutandis
as the scientists didn't reciprocate
with a series of lectures, puh, puh, puh,
lacklustre contra echo-locating the numbers,
furtive zhee notes fronting the shirt
& extensive slurring, a tendency to take
air, note-ending as if, & gradually
the twink & tseet & the tupe of the group
looking up, & thumbing the index
for a collective, localities of Moscow
where Promptoff might be phrasing
coelebs or gengleri, as each is composed
of what? Or silence for the speaker,
Cage all busy and whistling on or out
of his elbow—ho, ho, ho, all surreally
gestating silence as if words aren't enough—
fuck his submissiveness and things
always going wrong like the apocrypha
carnivore head & shoulders consumed
by the rest, frequently imbibing
basilar membranes with efficiency
out of tune with their size: take
Chrysotis amazonica, subsong,
mnemonics catchcrying
acclamations of authenticity,
the word, the boring shock troops

re-meta-cascando or The First Anniversary

8 lines from samuel beckett's "Cascando"

in their trash can or on
       their bench
assemblages
in their bench or on
         their
trash can someone
discover territorials
and assemblages
in zones of borrowed
       refrain

1.   why not merely the despaired of
the break itself seems too unreal & only we perform
as publically taught (we should), wherein or
so expected: just as good to have someone
tell the storm

2.   occasion of
a reconciliation which must happen
before the ceremony as consent gives totality
to this our considered **disaster**: Polaroids
are much cheaper than a pro-photographer

3.   wordshed

when only the letters in their utterances
mean: the sound of your voice indecipherable,
a single word as on the banks the sandbags
mount against the flood, rarely *ha!*
the Avon broken into the town, over the growing
lands. in England "creek" is a bit of a joke.

4. is it not better abort than be barren

Woke with new wife. Stepchild watching television.
But there is no means of production,   ~~profit~~   in the air.
The photograph configurations on the wall have
                        changed. Some
            new objects, the rifle
once busily downing parrots no longer visible. The old
green falcon utility is still
up on Taylor's Road near the tank-on-its-side—school
                        busstop—the
salt's diminishing & the crops thickening. The contour
                        banks
have worn down a little more & it looks as if one of
                        those neglected
disc-ploughs in the top paddock has been resurrected.
            The season
is blatantly fertile. There even seems to be fewer car-
casses   in the "sheep's graveyard".

5.   the hours after you are gone are
            so leaden
that I collapse under the weight of my own demons,
no longer placating rejecting or dispensing
with yours
                without whom dispossession draws else-
                                where,
where they are needed.

6. they will always start dragging
            too soon

like the legs of a heron locked in flight
that of the air is so physically different
too us outside assumed
as the knowledge it represents
though concerns only itself
as
references subverting the read text
of the preened body
as commodity
& the need to touch feathers
as the ode liberates
& the flight is oppressed
by the rhythm:
the bird contrived itself
                unique
though lost corrupt
its surplus speech,
as the uttered sound deep
in paperbarks
the water mirror black

deflected our indifferent fears
unless we relate it to our mood,

the bird is a bird
and the story builds
& is genuinely strange
and the bird is political
in and only in our usage
absolute
in language,
sound collation
IS the whoop of the swamp
as we migrate
within outed areas
without encroaching
or creating borders
with specific
communications.

7.　the grapples clawing
　　　　　blindly the bed of
　　　　　want

imposed against the vengeful's
suffering at the hands
of conscience, a parasite with hooks
imposing, dousing down the costly linen
spread like a drop sheet
over a particular
　　　shyness

8. bringing up the bones the old loves

jiggered in the rattle bag of divination
memory nothings the pleasantries: up
the snowy egret majestic in the hazy skies

but breathing deep the air is clear:
such a bird clots on a metal frame,
a sinecure: that deity as light—
contracepted—as deeper
than deep the diggings
cure!

alterity

poems without tom raworth

On the flats
they take their cues
as if wave-lengths
had intoned
latent rhythms
as emerge bones
from beneath the embryo:
a regional
phenomenon or
migration across
the fertile load;
tensed in the room
it might chain,
might genetically
play up, or play it up,
this small drama
of reception
some call incursion,
or settlement

but, the inhalation
takes the passive
by surprise as deep within
the polypus uncoils,
like Autumn's
big hit on the silver screens,
snakes alive! and down there
where the others are,
snake-handlers swing taipans
like bullwhips, cracking
against original night,
as if the like were punishment
for catching strains
of a popular tune,
the lingering signs
of assimilation

vestigial nights
upped the covers and lay low
lady day as if she had a say
in the compilation of the tale;
Richard Burton—heart aglow
translating peignoirs
and othering New-York:
sans refrain stretching
Ingres and tobacco stains,
ticker tape swirling gratis,
headlining coils
of dead sea scrolls,
sumptuous summonings
heavy in the lazing stomach—
having had nothing
to do but digest
the painted scene

so he bit back,
off-loading the slur,
an auger lifting his seed
into clouds which up till then
had refused to yield,
slick as Conrad
in a Polish sea,
pragmatic
as Artaud's naïvetté
bringing us closer to Foucault,
counter-clockwise
on the gibbet, casting
judgement and lurking behind
the Mason-Dixie Line,
his photographer
taking up the rear

into realms of kudos,
scrutineers sundered on bright-
sided volcanoes, sacrificial
in hissing light, moss
agitating on the far sides
presumably; click click
go village castanets
and we all bolt South
beyond the Brussels lace
of Spring, or out of Paris—
estivage—dragging the whole
stretch into our lungs,
sublime and redolent
with debauch and paradigms,
awkwardly glacial

clues & glass
double-take the Ranter
makeshift in his cabinet,
sparingly additive
in the breakers
rolling extraneously
against International Klein Blue
shores, pseudo-surfing
the readymades and getting lost
in the thickening soup;
come and join our narrative
the lush Catholic says,
gender hidden beneath a cassock
reeking of XY chromosomes,
it's as obvious as that

le train-train quotidien
en correspondance pour
the feast, sumptuous on tracks
busy with blood, overawed
in Frans Snyder's larder-studio,
jeopardy and deception
inciting swollen melons
as if the whole spread
was for him to get
his teeth around,
the master's dirty weekend
a riot, scum
nibbling at his sticky fingers,
the penis function
unitary and determined
to break free, in spite
of semioclasty

per obituaries
of arms inventors,
clips blooming—yes, like roses,
urges syncopated
in a towering narrative,
instrumentality undoing
targets stuck on the tracks,
pennies flattened into
dull planets upsetting
the currency balance,
revolving for us,
emancipating the uncomfortable
in their rotten boroughs
as the trans-Siberian lurches past,
indifferent to hubristic
proclamations bellowing
from the sleek guts
of the flying
Scotsman

lancing him
with their eyebeams,
panopticonian crossfire
conjuring holograms—
flak booming against
the big top like Brahms
auditing the Star Chamber,
racketeering body parts
with an energy Shelley
might have brought
to muster, at dusk,
the long-horned steers
grazing about billabongs,
a chopper cutting up
the stramineous
remains of a bull-
market Sun

it's the patterning
between orbits
harrying the cross-
dresser, busy within
the eyepiece, scanning
an aching vista,
colluding with frost
and sun, pinpointing
a vanishing point
on the artificial horizon,
remaining an imperative
echo or operative:
the new machine
churning out
ten thousand
Virginia blends
per minute, second,
or never

the curve narrow
and the spy planes
wire controlled,
displaying missives
like Black Mountains,
so precious and woebegone,
alternating across
the field like saturnine
demi-devils, busy
being matinee idols,
lounging in excruciating
banana chairs and caring
greatly about the adjectives
worn on their tanned shoulders
(yes, _like_ epaulettes)
all hunky and thin
at once

out of mazurka
incoherently squabbling
all-too-straight paradigms
& cataclysms, mendacious
climbings up the sanctioned
peaks, outwearing
winkle-pickers in the odious
airs of the subway,
metro, or U-bahn, fundamentally
disagreeing with agents provocateurs
and the makers of semtex,
high priests big-noting
the Underground while
opposing the jitterbug,
outing zoot-scooters

reduced to lampooning
marginal seats,
casting mug-shots
and gloating
like a thumb-nail moon,
all agitating in the limelight
and exposing the tenets
of basic English; they
pulled down the blinds
in the wagon-lit
and perspired rapidly,
gasping their way
through wads of language,
end-stopping and bursting
with doctrine

but then, what do you expect, out there on the islands?
conversant atolls
narrowing the scope of their dialogues, overgrown
with polyps and trumpery,
jealous of the water lens in the coral aquifer,
Charles Darwin busy
on the Beagle, quipping with his pen as it maps
yet another chapter
in the history of coral reef formation, and the Russians
already on the periphery,
nosing about like they own the world, and this the goddamn
Indian Ocean, the tides
full-on off Sumatra, and the lazy-boys floating
like navigation aids
amongst the troughs and crests and mute guests
and death wishes,
the whole time the horizon burning specifically
a whizz bang gadget in the General Electric
kitchen, getting off
on the trills of an abrupt finish, the only item left
being Derrida's letter z

yes, outside came the rhetoric
of wheels on the pavement,
centrifugal and vaguely specific

as rosellas exploded their disorderly
palette, shattered a Widow Maker's
foliage, the Freo Doctor scarcely

rustling up a critic on the banks
of the river, another pylon
driven into the head of the Wagyl, ranks

of police charging 'brightly coloured' protesters;
the narrative of isolation
unfurling relaxedly, agitators

safely stowed in the lockup, deaths black like fumes
that might also be parrots
while the clock on Winthrop Hall looms

large in the day of government's gritty
computers, translating worldspeak
and connecting the discourse, the city

sharp in the sunlight, coasting
towards desiccation—a ruse
to make outsiders think its beaming

countenance is pluralistic,
that kangaroos do hop freely on the freeways,
rehearsing their national trick

from The Echidna Project

Echidna

for Jacques Derrida

Rhythmically burrowing up on the toproad
in the graded remainders, the swampy contours
that look good for digging, that you'd
like to get amongst and smell—
those substratas, more than dirt and roots,
rhizomic agendas of the feeble-eyed,
uttering-up refrains from where
compactness and density
are demarcation and territory,
where decaying mallee root
or corpse of storm-felled Wandoo
tan the leathery bag of muscled fluid,
the flow of ants as white as Moby Dick,
as determined against the pulpy hull of trees
as against the gridded surface. Down where
the highway is sensed in the movement of sand-
particles, the hérisson—istrice in Italian,
in English, hedgehog—excavates
determinedly. At risk, this bristling heart
litters the roads with dedication,
symbols of the national psyche
left to bloat in the sun's blistering
prosody: inseparation that mimes
mechanics on the surface: ‹by heart›,
that without footnotes is still recognised
as the source of all under-movings.
I consider as memory tracking an echidna
with a farmer in Jam Tree country—
locating the spirit of place,
as if its being curled in a tree hollow
might validate the vast spread
of open tillage—but struck
by a kind of amnesia we wandered
in a circle tight as a fist, exhuming
the deeply choric question of rendering

our meanderings into prose,
into idle chatter to accompany
a few beers in the pub that night;
the portfolio of our imagined data
presented with detachment
as the slow-moving underminer
of our confident lyrical selves
fed ravenously,
deep in the heart
of the forest.

Amnesty Echidna Manifesto

Among fostered overtones
they skip the elegy
and wonder if the Wet is written
down like sinusoidal spirals
in the cosmology of specimens—
pages vigorous with nostalgic yearnings,
as the question is asked—that Amnesty
need make commentary
on a "civilized" Australia?
From the fat of denial
secreted milk oozes
onto the membrane
of the pouch, like Frank Thring joking
that he'd make a tobacco sac
out of the bush ranger's scrotum,
as spines erupt and the music
of weaponry is struck
by musing policemen, as there's
no way out of borrowed text
and the fossil record
is but a single external opening
focussing sex and excreta,
this the profit, the artefact
and its market, depositing eggs
and suckling progeny
on milk; and this a dialogue
of singing and witnessing
over the poem's anatomy,
as if other factors have crept
into a consideration
of an echidna opening
Meat Ant mounds
with inspirational claws,
deeply snouting and colluding
and outing cases of fixed-format

languages, conferring heritage
only after the fact,
as if it matters, as if subentries
to an apparently neutral hibernation
are of the place, like naming
names and collecting data
from "I've lived amongst them"
observations: in the lock-up
they observe "primitive" objections,
knowing better in their justice,
making comparisons, saying
"like an echidna" she bristled
against the "apparent" rape—
the Ombudsman declaring
as bold as Achilles
that he'd take the day,
forgetting always
that the murky water of the Styx
hadn't covered his glowing skin
entirely, and that in those parts
no-one had heard
of that river

Quill

quill or spine in the egglaying
recoil into the bristling
or "almost impenetrable
shield of lances"
in the home country's
curiosity, in its
urge to collect and label,
that centrally hollowed rib,
those birds of a feather
ground-bound and digging
heavily, if rapidly, in;
in the elevation, the rate
of azimuthal change
might remain constant,
despite the snout or beak
downing the tree of life,
getting in under the roots,
declaring colonies and empires
of white ants,
Schnabeligel, or maybe
the winged-down South
of the lighter-than-it-appears
hérisson, or than appears
in the summery arc of the sun,
the eye dependent on burning
as the final layers of scrub
are peeled back or frazzled
in the orderly, the controlled
burn,
      all steady below the water table
or above the artificial horizon,
deep in the vertical canals,
atop the cones of termites,
immediate and phylogenetically
related, like the quill of a crow

absorbing the black ink,
marking the white page,
staining the spread
like echidna droppings
per the continuum
of most sovereign communications:
the subsoil proving rocky
proving that a quick tongue
won't eroticize
the traumatic,
that de Sade is really popular
reading and delved
in the velocity of a bursting
timber, the libertine flames
ogling the circadian rhythms
of protected species,
the red velvet plushing
the imitative theatre,
minimally separable,
minimally *c'est le feu qui se relève avec son damné*
as if the law firm
confirmed a mating season
with the navigational accuracy
of a quill driven
by no hand
alone, by no hand
in conjunction with
se *hérisser* (of hence *hérisson*)—pen or poil
not held at the correct
angle, the penknife
rending stratas
of intonation
and several metaphors: stands
of mallet rib a vaulted
I K B sky, bound

together by the protein
lactotransferrin,
ah, *J'ai embrassé l'aube d'eté*
translated back—*un piquant!*—
against the beaked
and opened
anthills, the quill
and manuscript

Odour

The *short-nosed spiny anteater is a loner and usually territorial, occupying an area measuring about 2500ft (800m) in diameter, which overlaps with the patrol areas of others of their species. It is still unknown whether a home range is used exclusively by only one animal. These animals, with their well-developed sense of smell, can probably recognize each other "personally".*

ENTRY IN ENCYCLOPAEDIA

In the calm, sign-posted bush
   rhythms
   of burrowing
emit a specific odour
and patrols are profit-driven,
     and
exploitive, a farmer planting
plantation trees
   on the outskirts
is neither here nor there
when the canker
   hits the heart
   and termites
run veins
     through
their anatomy;
    here or there
we might enter the territory—
nothing personal
    though an echidna
curled up
   by a jamtree
   elicits
a genetically imprinted reaction:
hey,
    take a whiff of this!

they named this place
after your grandfather,
    and recorded his mark
    on the map; hey, note
the bush's timbre—
            the breeze cutting up the leaves,
tractor out & about
    in the open spaces—
        beyond
    the plumes of wood smoke—
spilling its guts
    in turmoil, its radio blaring full-blast
as if this popular music has a bouquet
as if you could eat it
    [*dans l'odeur chaude des galettes, des baguettes et des babas* . . .]
as if you could marry its smell to the taste
    of the bush—the biscuit-coloured dryness of summer
        covering the trenchant tracks
of the echidna,
    precisely—within 800
        or 1600
            metres,
above sea level

Echidna Photomontage
for JD

Sign wastage is not quill-written,
though feather might visually
correlate—we ask if it's been
hollowized, or tacked down
like skin on a hunter's drying
board—a medley of trouble spots
of this supplanted eschatology.

miniature savage technical growth
in an aquatic dry—urchin, anemone, porcupine fish,
crown of thorns starfish chewing away
at the Great Barrier Reef—adequatio;
style value? or rupture? to engrave
to save to colloquialize the grave—
memory of plough cutting its way

through paddock, through scrub,
pre clearing, when echidnas grubbed
for termites, found rabbits at wandoo roots;
it's that simple, we might call it abbreviation,
a ceremonial technique: nuzzling, bristling, cutting
three dimensions like growth—
boustrophedon, with no references

beyond its limited territory. the sky
metallic blue, favouring neither left
not right as vantage point, return
to disk operation, an orientation of quartz
and gravel finds, tracked roller, war machine
imposition, as if habitation and class distinction
are required—protected with a magic pen,

serial number kept on file at police stations.
it's about retaining social independence.
noxious influence spiked with hubris—
where the third eye travels, I will go.
Its appearance a fact, not necessary.
Sand and rock and wry vegetation.
The risk of extinction. Graphically speaking.

The Cars That Ate Paris: A Romance

"A la fin tu es las de ce monde ancien"
GUILLAUME APOLLINAIRE

for Peter Weir

Carboygirl, carboyalpinegirl, carcokeboyalpinegirl,
wheeloff on a bend, crushed car cokegirl alpineboy
splotches on fred williams' landscape, new automobiles
here become ancient

sign, sign shell, sign on
for the Commonwealth Rural Employment Scheme
co-sine, workplace
agreements, the road leads to mainstreet,
tucked in denuded hill-pieces

9 is the car rego,
nine the time it takes to engender
F-models and brothers, big oil
price rise coming,
primed like a canvas

do you take coupons?
gallons of coupons, two:
these country roads
these country roads
do you, drive out
fresh air, glide

a dark night
a few with his evening meal
a few, where shadows
might go, failed to take
the bend in the valley
of shadows, more
than a few, a few
too many: parrots out there
even if we don't
always hear 'em

red cross drills
Corolla
186—doyenne of six cylinders, lovely red rocker cover, high
   climber of hills,
higher than prayers, notes sprung from windscreens shattering,
devilish Toyoglide...

tests, tests on you: screen tests on you

on He, nothing's to be touched,
touched as guest, host with your name on it,
out here in the country, Les is a fierce car, not pierce
but verged and falling,
nothing's to be touched:
more ops for research, the country hospital where they patch
   you up
after accidents. the nurse your craning neighbour, priest-doctor-
   fly paper inscriber,
as arrived by machine in fraternal crowds
nothing's to be touched:
to become
a Parisian, a Parisian

Gilds
Notre-dame
Vie or via
Undercurrents of
British
Petroleum

car   television   two cars   smash
"accident"
horse   ball   scissors   cow
          Accident

Gosh Lord, sometimes you work in ways
that are totally incomprehensible, sometimes
your work, sometimes Lord,
totally

idle youth as lazy
as work they idle, engine-idle,
idle as flywheels
unworked, as an American President,
who what was, his name was,
Deal? His new Roosevelt: get them
to work, be upright as signs

our visitor, we're keeping him

I have to wear it in the house,
he won't let me wear it outside:
in-house, outerwear hangs out

lights mention a scene, of accident,
of feral eyebites in black pitched
down a tone,

knocked that old man down, those pedestrian
aged problems, up and down, life, this yo yo
moonwalk: interpolation

acquitted but not driving, no longer:
the state road toll at an all-time high
and I reaching, reaching to drive
out

O Jaguar, robbing the corpse,
to pay Peter, O the need for big fingers
to play Chopin or boogie those dance beats,
O light piano, curst flameburst,
cremated

in the car cemetery: here, a pastoral of the dead:
the grave of ransom subtle in well-kept aside,
young pacified: a white tomb as bright
as sunlight of Paris, sword-crosses, armfuls of wildflowers?
of metal twists, coronets of rust
gleaming all the same: pioneer stock

roadworks, power poles, realtime
insignia: Lescar, foiling
figuratives and escapes: I am
a plane man, a plan man
without fancy pants,
fancy wordplans...

twodeathsonconsciencefeargod
fearbellevue ward fear of

the world of motorcar
carma

you have your full vegies, half vegies, quarter vegies
PAL
they told me about George they told me about George
they told me about George
they're orphans
they're orphans not ours
those lights seen on the night
of the accident,
lowland swamp oil-film rustwater
black out of heart they fear

cars encircle howitzer
Rock of Ages
407
demo derby as I saw the French Hell drivers when I was a kid
and DID sing onward Christian soldiers
as a neighbour collected jaguars
and emblems like fetishes,
his son growing dope and playing electric guitar
in cover bands
of note

ha ha ha he he he
Paris Pioneer Ball
don't I love thee . . .
manifest past in two holy holies
in bountiful presence like Paris old town old Paris,
these bounties, and youth derby steam letters
epiphanies to future, these progeny, cataphiles
beneath streets of very blue skies,
pastures-no, arrondissements-of sharp sunlight
and dead cows assisted into car trunks: remember that?

quasi eucalypti wreckages
mirror enlightenment and rational
dazzling, as wrecked in chevs, old trucks on farm
that grow grizzled, express lachrymose ideations:
NSW BNS 973
as something misses in family, our familiars,
the son, trinity, to settle
yourself family, part of family,
this closest of families wouldn't do unto others
as talk, as outsiders take our chatter,
take our talking like pioneers
wouldn't, who'd settled this land
seizing—we have to—opportunities,
all orphans coming help-seeking,
regenerating
Parking Officer, esteemed dignitary, black arm-patched

into community, into crepes
at the Eiffel Tower Café, oh
machine of the century, modernity
international, telling us to park here and not there
as revenge broods in a generation snapping: the Mayor's
Aborigine broken in half: a warning, a warning to all the people
who defy the laws of Paris: burning, Les-burning,
clasp your goolies on this, this burnt-up
technology

the priest's collar,
collar of blood,
the good bits
kept always
to yourself

through hard days and costumes
victories come Nobody, Nobody
leaves Paris: CHINAMAN, AFRICAN MISSIONARY,
cabinet: Arnott's Bikkies, Rice Bubbles, LadiesandGentlemen
FellowPioneers, ticked by cruel fate
midst taken, mist of spirit
still with us, the grave
of a pioneer: light, light at the end
of the tunnel, short distance
remaining

woomera woomera quandong billabong emu wallaby kanga-roo
quandong woomera emu woomera woomera wallaby kangaroo
woom-dong-bong-u-rooquawallabongroomu

t's the cars,
it's the cars
they're a bit upset,
a bit upset
over the burning

German Explorer, Early Missionary, Joust

Pig shield people's wagon sat mace, the joust, the joust!

Upset cars ramraid joust weirdly melancholic, grotesque:

No safe road out, no safe road, no dance safe...

I can drive Edith Piaf, I can drive out of Paris

I can drive through
the evacuation
of Paris, drive-thru
tears of refugees
vacating
the shabby ruins
of Paris

[389]

filmed at Wattle Flat.

Recent Poems

Transgenic Pig Ode

Pig, heart-bred, is clean in its stall,
almost clinical, and ambivalently
sexual, glowing DNA that genealogically
connects with the Earl of . . . and a fair-minded
radical, a dissenting minister . . . or a famous
female novelist not read now . . . and back *then*,
strands of tribes recorded as cannibals,
a swatch of hair or skin
hijacked from the museum,
decoded, set in motion over again
as the patient with pig-heart blooms
in hospital, grateful to the donor pig.
Pig grunt equals words vaguely scientific,
or Babelistic, as in the lab-shed
their cousins, decked up on stainless
steel and plastic scrubbed to the point
of futurity: "We", they gleam, "stagger
towards immortality!" We are
clean at heart, *Cor Cordium*,
when in Rome . . . exorcise
religious tolerance, overcome public
discomfort like the early years of tobacco
advertising, valves opening and closing
like discourse; hey, you visualise
sties maintained by an uncle,
wallow pits and straw sacks,
laid-up sow with a litter of squeals,
and the runt with whom we
bi-sexual poets identify, this ode
to Swinburne and pig-fucking:
the Euro sex-industry argues
it's near the real thing, perfect
simulacrum of human: bio-ethically,
can this be held up for scrutiny? Sexual feeding-
frenzy as the gut barrow is emptied,

sheep carcass swinging in the shed,
cleaned hollow, pigs profiting
and putting weight heavily
into Anglican collection bowls.
That's home town self-sufficiency.
A neighbour ran pigs intensively
and their skin was so pink beneath the tin roof
and fluoros. The stench out back
wasn't mentioned at party meetings
but came up as an ethical issue at town
council—the five mile drift.
In forests of the Darling Range feral pigs
snout roots of hardwood, upturn humus,
bristle and call big-balled tuskers to charge
the hunter: hollow-pointed bullets
that split the skull, explode in hearts
they'd carry round as trophies,
these clean fair liberties,
these pulses and throbbing auras
we project as animal selves,
remove surgically and place delicately
in chambers of destiny.

Seed Ethics

a composition for Blixa Bargeld

tacit
effulgency
        opening
original, spliced
about cape tulip
salvation jane (dry season, starting point—
        these celebrations)
intracity and germinal, assonance
in-drill, briefly under
surfaces, capital
works, growing on
trees
type
space between rows
cast, winnowed,
old variety bright
in shadow of: buffer,
cloistered, sharp canola
infused

swift, heron, crow
deterrent endings
decorate; see us
in housing—foundations
coated, frosted,
wastes all about,
sweetpea struggle, grow
to make less vulnerable
tomatoes and trysts
lessened to lengthen
shelf-life, this half-life
        odeless tomato
interphased, bottom-dwelling

[395]

fetishist up-ended
before
        the committee
        think tank

cessate despite
exponential runoff
tagged as sunflowers taking
just, we walk through insects,
beneath planes and trailings
        earth moving
lymphocytes, glandular...
ostic

juice. exfoliate cavities
chambers the seedless, we of the polis
employ mercenaries; we subscribe
its resistance
        defoliant;
marvel intestate, corporate,
superstitious

to boutique sufferers
I offer none, rose syn.,
railside, anti-salinists
warning against salt-
        creeping
                into their houses,
love less, less germinations,
pre-deceased
an I-prayer articles barren ground;

[396]

inculcates tracks and gastronomes
in plant dress: hemp shirts
unbleached vestments;
    less hot these chillies
    down through generators,

strata, plurals, hooks
in quarantine hindsights,
hinterland fostering
hypo
    thesis

the rooster
synonymically dead to a fox
redrafted as prejudice
in small bound town
of citizenic hymnals,
mourning services,
mourning we here community,
    as connected
folk object to Aboriginal Studies,
    object to boys playing netball,
eat wild oats selectively taken,
downtrodden spray recipients
saying it's necessary

weaker strains of day pullulate
as manifestoes in antipodean poetry;

stinkweed wreaths national fortune
fortitude, luck . . . interiority:

AKA spinifex, award ceremonies,
lab noises,
        heart protests
suppressed
largesse

phenoxy herbicides
down weeds
in wheat crops

a lack of soil mobility
endears, ingratiates, fraternises
roots, culture of roots,
as half enough colloquial
to vernacularise gossip and lies,
global prospects;
        in-stagnantly, alluvial semaphores
of dyadic heraldry, dynamic estuaries,
stray mangroves
swamped. but that's in the north...
ablative absolute broccoli
not rotting or dusting yellow
declass? perish thoughts
of justice, perish lawful levels
        of vitamins & minerals;
not impoverished
by toxins?
audience: biological
therapeutic, prospective

the committee
was hygienic and bountiful
prudent and generous
aesthetic and lush
linear and lateral
comprehensively dialectic, binding
nomenclature like nodules of nitrogen
to correct orders and patina, bountiful
forward
      planned innovation
and cautionary tailings

appeal to prod openness
deaf-eared grain-glow
underwritten like
warfare; and rodents
in fields concomitant
and doubly negative

after a warm day a cold change
comes over us: on the weather
discussion list
      racism & patriotism
phase in;
      cloned from embryos
these internal wars, as pre and pretà
as lightning,
its shape

runner beans will climb
as staked against snow
and here, hellish temperatures,
coaxed kitchen, wild flowers
papered to walls by numbers,
dish fallen
within our fields,
error zones intoning
lavish principles,
hardship tracking
strains of, vagrancy, portraiture, 2-4-D,
the lupins disguising healing portfolios,
those thin and fleeting fetishes

Graphology 8—speech training and transcription

Item, we know
the fire in my room,
we feel impervious; an excursion
through town, past a friend's rooms
in St John's, where he's not
because on weekends
he's invariably out
at Granchester.
Should we know him there,
as we know this fire?
Should we "feel"
what we see
in others' frames
of reference?
Like trusting translation,
or that a script
will be read right
by the pharmacist.
Like believing in jargon.
Asking: will the swan's nest
yield again next season?
Will the swans nest
in the old nest.
The nest will still be,
maybe empty,
falling to bits.
Either way, the apostrophe.
We watched daily
for the hatching—just a quick glance,
so as not to disturb.
A spectacle. We made
conversation of it. Some—probably many—
took notes. Hand-written.
Or in their electronic notebooks.
Working for a scientific future

the conference
exceptional
immaculate
sans serif
as neat as a button
loveless but lusty
pissed and well fed,
unleashed conjecture,
unleashed swallows about the tower
of St John's chapel
darting like small fish
in a bright light
shone from the jetty above.
This is gratuitous, there's no need for comparison,
it goes anywhere and everywhere and is quantum
in its explication:
boustrophedon. The grammatical map
supplied herein is neither here nor there.
You know now the pace is presto!
How fast have you been reading or speaking this?
It is written: the hand chaotic, agitated.
Just to get it all down! Letters open, disconnected,
serifs obscuring the words in the line
below, and below that. An interest
in IBM golf balls, of various fonts,
wiped out the uncial notebooks of youth,
the temporal features: those wandering dots.
Pixel-dropout.
. . . . .
. . . . .
. . . . .
. . . . .

What we see through my eyes
in the hazy light: a lone oak tree

becomes the memory of York gums and jam tree: the red sap
like jam, you see. Place-layering
is tension, confusion.
The place is neither
here nor there.
It is a place I know,
like Russell knowing the earth
he walked on.
I know we know. We know I know I,
we know. We. We, I know.
Do we compare the chortle
of an English magpie with the warble
of an Australian (one)? They are both
black and white. That is the nature
of sound, a gloss
on varieties of the infinite,
a rough boy's speech,
a fin de siècle house style,
locked-boxes in the archives,
temperature controlled,
not overdoing the oeuvre,
tears at the end of a biography
of someone you might
well have despised, their being real
neither here nor there,
and what I know of that tree
is littered at its base, seasonal change
coming on fast, erupting
almost, the piano in the chapel
atonal on atonal,
if we could do away with cultural specificities
of words in the Trinity, if it could
float on air, this pain so shallow,
tawdry decoration,
charity and temperance,

a social responsibility
not to get too big for your boots
in a context you despise—
wouldn't say a bad word
but hope the whole lot falls
down around your ears,
the oprahfication, the olympicisation,
accountability, authenticity, virtue
and free speech: holarctic,
to stitch up and the last Kray
is just out, a burly man on the door
of his cheap hotel, they'd have you care,
air strained in columns, polite talk not messed up,
distorted, dialect and accent,
down on tap: transcribed
what Villon might transcribe
in the blue-blood's book, widows
and orphans encrypted, or a philosopher's
childhood code

                    . . . . .
                    . . . . .
                    . . . . .
                    . . . . .
                    . . . . .

in the country, gold medals
for a duck-rabbit kill,
sports and belles lettres
feed the city, a tag sprayed
on a roadside, identity,
church-rage, refugee,
refuge, the white cliffs of Dover,
detention centres Down Under,
the art critic's Australia,

the Coming Back of expatriates
temporarily, Australia's Year
of Autographs, lodged, detached,
judged, asseverate exploded consonants
as if "word power"
makes drug cheats discrete,
as if piglets with human proteins
give a grunt, press-cleaned,
glowing excrement: an ink, of sorts,
across the walls, through the bars
of the cot. Observe the matrix:

Medal Count

Country	G	S	B	T
United States	20	12	18	50
China	17	11	11	39
Australia	10	16	11	37
Russia	08	08	12	28
France	10	10	05	25

Change is written all over it:
investment, colour,
weight, numerology,
currency, topology,
geography, economics,
social welfare,
infrastructure,
language death.
The pace becomes ponderous: grave.
Paterson's curse plagues the property
and yet its purple effusion
in late-winter is something
to behold. It is the driving memory

here, for us. It is what we see
written in my notebook: "curse"
is underlined, heavily
scored, proof
of nothing . . .

Graphology 9—a declaration and the paper it is printed on

Lacking personality traits
he adopted a mode of handwriting
that he might call his own—a sample
from a book, a stray piece of paper
with a quick reminder note,
something caught his eye.
The mimesis was total
and once adopted
there was no turning back—
he wasn't, in fact, a born
forger, just a damn-near-perfect
facsimile. People
reacted to the good and the bad
in him, and he could see
right from wrong
in a way that had been
previously denied.
"I have gained character
through script," he'd say,
refusing the keyboard,
always preferring to use
pen and paper. He took his skills
to his left hand as well, just reversing
the slant. As if to stimulate
a neglected side
of identity.
Writing the same thing
with both hands: the black bird—a crow—
is alone on the green lawn, beak
taking in the last light,
focused in the place
where roots grow.
Curiosity grew stronger,
and a desire for a genealogy
to go with his identikit

had him draw up
his family tree: it
mapped his hand's history,
gave him a past:
a ballerina, an opera singer,
a poorly paid landscape artist,
a military man who was lost in India,
a number of petty bureaucrats,
a cigar manufacturer,
a preacher from a dissenting church,
a swag of colonists and teachers,
a suicide, a seamstress
and a piano teacher.
A rich heritage: graphologically,
lower middle middle class; spiritually:
a carbon copy, a signatory
to a bill of rights, a constitution,
a health & wealthy
first-world democracy—
well armed and ready
to go, collateral
and federal, progressive
and centralised,
"local and global";
the paper he wrote upon,
most often white.

Graphology 11

The pathology of a cyber is under-
written rhetoric and scriptic hijinks,
ascii punnage, as old as refrigerator magnets
oughtabe, says, lan'sakes, say a blot
on the record, that periodicity,
confounded omni-speak, such a
conference: that 'tranny' hand,
and/or general anaesthetic
making hands shaky,
aesthetics dodgy,
as if change(d) might be measured
in the character of writing,
of Ohio cursive.
What do we have in sign?
What ligature and sinew
in panoramics, the director's
cut of straw dogs or the like,
land, and place, vineyards
in full Virgil, this bodymass,
this tattooing self and calling
it cultivation. No farmers,
no food, it says. We eat
our own inscriptions.
A platitude. An aphorism. Lacunae.
Note in waste spaces, frame
those sleepy mappings. In these robin-rich
carbon-dioxide absorbing
green tailings, as if rhythms should bind,
hinted and spoken. So, this sovereignty,
and damn culture as viable,
incremental as blazes, stunning
as headlines, straight
from the hellbox. Hot as type
cast, and ink vats. That's what comes
of electronic fonts and references.

What can I write for you?
That you were here, order
in front of me, of my eyes: chickencoop,
freerange quillage, cabbage red lozenges,
all excuses for input, side effects:
pleasuring.

+

so, hot-to-trot, no more than we
were painted, enraptured and well-mannered,
this changing of the disposition: see

footprints and seals, good standard
raised at the table, as fidelity
implicates, not returned if tasted

+

In good society the legibility
of one's hand paramounts bonds
of marriage; in this quotation,
this ceremony, physiocratic portraits
no more candid than our childhood:
portions, upper tables, working words
like gluttony, or just hard to come by,
the spitting image. So ennobled,
he writes in crisis and disharmony
again. So might she. Sanctioned,
customs oftentimes intervened:
the elephant foot hat stand,
tigerbone stimulant,
bearskin rug.
Quarantine.
Bedlam.

Restrictions, prestige, luxury
items: souventes fois. Not in good company.
Spoken like a speech. Just
taking the disc plough for a burl,
cutting the top up, making patterns.
The scarifier fools no one.
Just plane vulgar.
Plain speaking, we make
sociology.

+

Visiting the house built by the third bishop of Ohio she said she knew
she had to behave, to be good. the view from that window
had to be kept intact, the trees topped just below
the sill, line-of-sight clean as a whistle,
she said he'd look out mid-epistle
to see the spire of his church.

+

None of the birds here are like or just as,
and the eye-pool compares to nothing:
sunless, they take light and deposit
droppings on the curl of the storm-fuelled
grass, which doesn't BELONG here anyway.
The state bird is a latecomer, they'll tell you.

+

Six times eighteen small panes inside six
larger frames, divisible by three larger frames,
three moving parts apart from latches.

+

Export sense and dissect
this rent, for God's sake, zoology and translation,
this echidna that projects
himself without giving herself
away: comprehension, cogency, universality.
Dead in the age it appeared in: now, that's
criterion. See, this life/death filial inscription,
see this remedy, borrowed decidable.
Effecting the product of paint, or produced effect
painted as newness, it creates hymn, creates city.
Night-hinged, plus je jet plume, reliure, door,
sepulcher: its buildings. Sexually
copperplate, as entailed as supplements.
This is for "yous" (differentiated
particles in class structures,
rabid defamiliarisation, they
wouldn't
                    even go there,
won't stream in the coastal town
of Geraldton). Vertical
literature is no crisis, like lists of flowers
(buddleia, irises, tic tocs)
spread into house,
the staged verandah,
a voter's registration.

I unsubscribe

mis demean our refuse
topped sub due, a lawn
and stippled verb, test
ice-top, signifiosis
stranger in private proprietory
cased in language
replies unrequested,
requiet paced across
sharp grassblades,
hypo, and where locate
geno flex ion buddings,
where petit declasse
testamental cultures,
columnular scroll, temples
and feathers parsed
odour, outré

why write no poetry more

estfavour, pour gramrare
incur, askew, aka insistentor
saqueneme est fixator
in, preser vert er stockist
clust, awed upclaw
un apologia, lyris
instignation, foreclose
upythesis, gerd luca
placirds, erd air,
syrios

& Succor

inist geothemies sistic, treple upclass -ments,
axiomies, I sest readentary: drinkables, thirst sents

func gigs up crites, less lovely, encircled festeries
can as can do, fuck hit'n duelists says groups, treez

On the Absence of the Actual:
Four Manifestations

1.

Fields without fences
promulgate: hills leaven
crests and lulls, fundamental
to families; tanks crenellate
pressure gauges, pipework, pumps
counterweighting sheets and hollows,
pressurepoints,
solid, liquid, gas: interchanges.

2.

Beavers pinpointing wetlands
to dam against hunter and farmer,
interiorising Candlemass;
groundhogs
charging shadows,
trashed on roadsides,
making TV appearances.
That youth camp in Mohican Forest—
a detention center, percussion
capping tension between canopy
of pines and birches, surreptitiously
splitting rocks, as far back
as an ice age.

3.

And here, in Holmes County,
the elongation of an error
backtracks prayer:
without electricity, despair
works salt and rain into highways,
and the atheist
believes diurnally.

4.

Narrowing from base
prospect of fire, lookout
towers over forest,
blind spots of redemption
make loss complex
in ice-growth,
so far below, shaped by vertigo
and the forest floor.

loy polloi love song

Commodious hosiery, that I tie
my white lies by, that I graft
to the bee with its pollen-shedding
undergarments; ah, flower farm
and laced integer, that by quotidians
of ten I mark profit, industry
I faithfully subscribe as Valhalla,
the hidden signature, the miracle
of the hole in the wall,
the popular art of thrust and shell-holes,
not scattered to industry. I love,
love out of reservoirs of ruby
and cybernauts, superculture
hand-held like the (s)trumpet-
attested waves of quietness,
that I—in my lair—hold out
against, auxiliary hairs
festooning velocipedes,
gibbets, labial undertakings.

ern via jk

Me: Down the Street, in the Park, 2000

Truncated, I switch a lock of grass
against the dominant posterior,
I twitch beneath a sun dark with smog
and pixels, I incite art-attacks in monument parks,
and make selection when squatters
turn their backs; understand this
my crepuscular love, as if I might
get your mood just right, these blowsy
gardens, transposed avenues. In tight pants—
stovepipes—you angle towards
my aural palette, and I hear your yelp,
cur-like, choked with crows and light.

ern via jk

Confessional without a tune

Detective love unstrings my package—
I'm left distraught on the verandah,
clutching a master's pinking shears,
the sun an orange sculpture freezing over
in tetra-paks and scummy dives.
A squirrel retreats into its dray,
and intrusion has me hard at it,
this rebel flesh concupiscent: lush
markets jacked up in the corridors
of the Louvre, glass pyramids reflected
in the Seine. Squeezing it shut
my saggy retrospect compacts, diminishes:
plucked breast whelping out of perspective,
scooters and ball games become skull-wadding.

ern via jk

Antidote

In-flux, rebuttal, spaced
about the jimmy, all weather
is typical, you said,
dressed in polymorphous heather.

I dreamt of recognition
in my own quiet spaces,
unmodulated microscopia,
the ephemera catching shoe-laces.

I exist, sum of phobias
and filaments — scunge
beneath the lip salve, naked
hearsay and bestial lunge.

An island mystery — tycoon
scrounging on the beaches,
credits and echoes trembling
as the hoot owl screeches.

Alone, I rage myself
with tribal valiance, I scoff
at the greatest writers,
and the verbiage of a conceptual toff.

In this bower, this mouldy shower
cubicle dank with history,
stuck-up pubes and awkward
queries conjugate my jury.

ern via jk

Dark Eclipse

It all started with uprightness,
this tendency to startle despite
a drift to the left: I waggle
in surplice schematics
criss-crossing the circuit boards
declaring diodes reborn,
come again in a silicon world.
Don't you want me
for my Gary Cooper nose?

Ah, Lilies of the Valley
that draw me up
by the short and curlies, popeye muscles
Scipio once admired, before some ol' bloke
retired. Spittle of Apollo, Maevius's scriptic tune,
a bloodtest pushed through the maiden's drawers.
I read him like a book on the smooth beach.
I betray not, the glory of unsettled usage,
the quatch-buttock. Suffer my command
in this, your period of duty — dressed up
in hose and flaunting imperial shoes.

Thrust in these damned wound-holes,
counteract my guest-host:
Ah, what's chivalry come to? Stop start,
gone to wars: attacking Frederick the Great.
The regular exception of night surprise:
mall survey, that propitious ray,
proximity of fame and name.
I was here, looking for you,
wind-thrummelled and all at sea
in my heavily starched sailor suit.

ern via jk